SCIENCE LOOKS AT MYSTERIOUS MONSTERS

Also by Thomas G. Aylesworth

STORM ALERT
Understanding Weather Disasters

Science Looks at Mysterious Monsters

Thomas G. Aylesworth

Julian Messner  New York

Published by Julian Messner, a Simon & Schuster
Division of Gulf & Western Corporation,
Simon & Schuster Building,
1230 Avenue of the Americas,
New York, New York 10020.
JULIAN MESSNER and colophon are trademarks of
Simon & Schuster, registered in the U.S. Patent
and Trademark Office.

Manufactured in the United States of America.

Design by Irving Perkins Associates

Second printing, 1983

Library of Congress Cataloging in Publication Data

Aylesworth, Thomas G.
Science looks at mysterious monsters.

Bibliography: p.
Includes index.
Summary: An inquiry into the nature of the
abominable snowman, Bigfoot, the Loch Ness monster,
and other monstrous creatures, the existence of
which has never been finally proven or disproven.
1. Monsters—Juvenile literature. 2. Animals—
Folklore—Juvenile literature. [1. Monsters.
2. Animals—Folklore] I. Title.
QL89.A94   001.9'44   82-2304
ISBN 0-671-43657-0   AACR2

CONTENTS

Looking for
MONSTERS

ON June 21, 1981, the *Washington Post* carried a news article concerning an upcoming African expedition. It was not a typical expedition in which the participants were out to shoot or photograph big game. Rather, they were going to look for a monster.

For 200 years, natives in the Congo had told of a giant reptile that remained mostly in the water and came to shore only in the early morning or at dusk to feed. The animal was believed to be a vegetarian, but it was said that it could become ferocious, and there were reports that it had killed several humans.

This ten-ton, forty-foot-long mokele-mbembe, as the natives call him, has been described as "half-elephant, half-dragon." The creature was also the object of a 1978 French expedition. The members of that search party were never heard from again.

The first time that people in the Western world heard of the monster was in 1913. A German explorer, Capt. Freiherr von Stein zu Lausnitz, reported hearing stories of a brownish-gray animal the size of an elephant, with a long and flexible neck and a muscular tail like an alligator's.

The American expedition left for Africa on October 25, 1981. It consisted of three scientists, a photographer, a missionary, and a security guard. They were to meet with ten Pygmy porters in the Congo and start their search.

The expedition was financed by Jack Bryan, a rich Texan, The National Geographic Society, and *Geo* magazine. The leader of the party was Dr. Roy P. Mackal, a microbiologist and tissue expert at the University of Chicago. He and his party were to travel on foot and by canoe, carrying with them antidotes for the poison used on Pygmy blow-darts, fourteen kinds of snakebite medicine, and a receiver that uses satellite signals to tell them their exact position in the jungle.

As it turned out, Mackal returned and announced on November 10 that he had not found the monster. But he did find huge footprints and a wide swath of bent and flattened vegetation. The tracks led into a river. The tracks were about the size of an elephant's, but the way that the brush was flattened suggested that the animal had a huge crocodilelike tail.

Did they really expect to find the monster? As Dr. Mackal said: "If skeptics say it's extremely unlikely, then I'm the first to agree. But it's not impossible. We've got to check out the long shots, because they pay off once in a while."

And that's the way many scientists feel about the possible existence of such creatures as the Abominable Snowman, Loch Ness Monster, Bigfoot, and many more. So far, they haven't been able to prove the existence of these beasts, but no one has been able to prove that they don't exist, either.

Actually, from a zoological point of view, the most elusive animals, regardless of size, are discovered last. The first to be observed are those animals that are most apparent in their environment. The most elusive ones may exist in areas in which humans do not usually find themselves, such as the depths of freshwater lakes or on the tops of remote mountains. In other words, they may be found in places that have not been adequately explored.

Perhaps we all should keep our minds open to the idea that strange creatures might exist in out-of-the-way places. And it's those strange creatures that this book is all about.

1

ABOMINABLE SNOWMAN

IN November 1951, two British mountaineers, Eric Shipton and Michael Ward, went 20,000 feet above sea level on the Menlung Glacier, which lies between Tibet and Nepal. It was at this point that they came across a trail of strange footprints in the snow. Each print was thirteen inches wide and eighteen inches long. And whatever made them had only four toes.

The footprints seemed to be fresh since they had not had time to melt. They were probably actual size, also, since a melting footprint tends to become larger.

The two men followed the trail for about a mile before the tracks could no longer be seen in the thinning snow. They took photographs. Many scientists who saw the pictures felt that the tracks could not have been made by monkeys, bears, or leopards—animals common in that area. The two inner toes seemed larger than the others, and the heel was broad and flat.

The London Zoological Society and the natural history department of the British Museum concluded, after looking at the photographs, that the tracks had been made by a langur monkey or a red bear. But this creature had walked on two feet. Bears can walk on two feet, but do not do so for more than a few steps, and are not known for leaping about snowfields on their hind feet. In addition, langur monkeys are small animals that walk on all fours. The stride of this mysterious creature was two and one-half feet between tracks and that, too, seemed to cast doubt on the monkey theory.

Then *The Lancet,* a highly respected British medical journal, came out on the side of Shipton and Ward. It published an article in 1960 which said that the existence of the beast might be possible.

What is this creature? The Tibetans call it the *Yeti,* which means "magical creature" in Tibetan. When newspaper editors first heard about it, they labeled it the Abominable Snowman.

The Sherpa natives of the Himalayan Mountain region claim to have seen Yetis. Some of them say that it is a small, squat animal the size of a fourteen-year-old boy with stiff red (or black) hair, a monkeylike face, and no tail. Others agree, but say that the beast is quite large. Most say that its feet are back to front with the toes trailing behind the heels.

The Yeti is so strong that it can throw boulders around

as if they were baseballs and uproot trees as if they were dandelions. Its body odor is horrible and would put a skunk to shame. The Yeti's voice has been described as a shrill whistle combined with high-pitched yelps and lion-like roars.

The Western idea of the Yeti's appearance is similar to that of the Sherpa's. Edward Cronin, a zoologist who has worked in the Himalayas, has combined all the descriptions and come up with his own conception of the beast. It is a stocky, apelike creature five and one-half to six feet tall with short brown or black hair covering all parts of the body except for the flat face. Huge teeth fill a large mouth. The head comes to a point. It has long, dangling arms, heavy rounded shoulders, and no tail. When faced with danger, it assumes an apelike, threatening stance.

By the early sixties, a system of classification of the Yetis had been set up. There were three types: the *Rimi*, which was up to eight feet tall and lived at altitudes of about 8,000 feet, the *Nyalmot*, which was fifteen feet tall and fed on mountain goats and yaks, and the *Rakshi-Bompo*, which was five feet tall and lived on grain and millet.

All three of these types of Yetis are shy and retiring. They come out at night and are seldom seen in groups of more than two. They like bowls of water and food to be left out where they can find them. The creatures, it is said, are also fond of alcoholic beverages.

Reports about the Abominable Snowman reached Europe as early as the mid-fifteenth century. But it was described in Chinese manuscripts that date back to 200 B.C. Supposed sightings of the Abominable Snowman and its tracks by people from the West go back to around the 1890s.

In 1889, Major L. A. Waddel of the Indian Army Medical Corps saw footprints of an unusual creature while he was mountain climbing in northeastern Sikkim. The footprints were found at an altitude of 17,000 feet. Waddel reported that he thought that they were the tracks of yellow snow bears.

In 1890, another mountain climber was exploring the slopes of Mount Everest on the Nepal-Tibet border. Measuring 29,028 feet in height, this is the world's highest peak. The climber told of discovering strange footprints at an altitude of 18,500 feet. The tracks, he said, led uphill and vanished among the boulders.

B. H. Hodgson, the British resident in Nepal in 1892, wrote an article about a mountain creature. It was an erect, tailless beast with shaggy black hair that had approached some Nepalese porters who promptly fled in terror. And who could blame them? These porters called the creature a *rakshas*, which is the Sanskrit word for "demon." Hodgson thought, however, that it was really an orangutan.

In 1914, J. R. P. Gent, the British Forestry officer in Sikkim, claimed to have seen some footprints. He thought that they had been made by some strange creature, and said: "Its tracks are about eighteen to twenty-four inches long, and the toes point in the opposite direction to that in which the animal is moving. . . . I take it he walks on his knees and shins instead of the sole of his foot."

The first time that a European claimed actually to have

seen a Yeti was in 1921. Lieutenant Colonel C. K. Howard-Bury led the first Everest Reconnaissance Expedition. He and his men were at an altitude of about 21,000 feet when one of his guides, a Sherpa, pointed to a figure moving through the snow. It was walking upright, and the Sherpas said that it must be the "Wild Man of the Snows."

In 1925, British photographer N. A. Tombazi supposedly saw the creature. Tombazi, a fellow of the Royal Geographical Society, was a trained naturalist. He was approximately 15,000 feet above sea level on the Zemu Glacier in the Himalayas when he spotted the Yeti about 200 to 300 yards away. Previously, he had been a disbeliever, referring to the legendary snowman as "that delicious fantasy." But his sighting caused him to change his mind.

"Unquestionably," he wrote later, "the figure in outline was exactly upright, and stopping occasionally to uproot some dwarf rhododendrons. It showed dark against the snow and wore no clothing." He later examined the footprints in the snow and described them in detail. They indicated that the animal was a biped.

The same Eric Shipton of the 1951 expedition saw his first Yeti tracks in 1936 at an altitude of about 16,000 feet. More snowman prints were found in 1937 by Sir John Hunt at 19,000 feet.

It is important to know that there are people who believe that the snowmen are not animals, but rather mystical hermits or solitary monks. And they are thought of as being kind.

One of the oddest confrontations between man and Yeti occurred in 1938. Captain d'Auvergne, the curator of the Victoria Memorial near Chowringhee in Calcutta, India, was traveling by himself in the Himalayas. He was becoming snowblind and suffering greatly from exposure, when a nine-foot-tall Yeti appeared. According to his tale, the creature carried him several miles to a cave and fed and nursed him back to health. Finally, he was well enough to return home.

The curator's theory was that the Yetis were really members of an ancient tribe, the A-o-re. Members of this tribe, it was thought, had gone to the mountains centuries ago to escape persecution, and evolved into giant, hairy beasts.

Slavomir Rawicz was a Polish prisoner in a Siberian war camp. In 1942, he and six comrades were able to escape and head home. They crossed the Himalayas to India, but on the way they supposedly met two eight-foot-tall creatures between Bhutan and Sikkim. They claimed to have watched the beasts for two hours from a distance of about one hundred yards.

Another story tells of two Norwegians who happened on two sets of tracks in 1948. They followed the tracks, hoping for a look at the strange creatures that they had heard and read about. Soon they came upon the Yeti that they claimed was responsible for the tracks. Figuring that if they brought the beast back alive, no one would doubt their word, they tried to capture it.

What the Norwegians are said to have done next is not exactly the approved way of capturing an Abominable Snowman. They tried to lasso it. This effort failed, but they came back down the mountain and reported that the Yeti looked like a large ape.

In 1953, Sir Edmund Hillary and his Sherpa guide, Tenzing Norgay, were the first men to reach the top of Mount Everest. On their way up the mountain they found giant footprints.

The London Daily Mail organized an Abominable Snowman expedition in 1954, but it was somewhat of a flop. The explorers came back with nothing but a few hairs from a 300-year-old scalp. The scalp was one of the treasures in a Buddhist temple and was supposed to have once belonged to a Yeti. It was eight inches high, the men said, and had a circumference at the base of twenty-six inches. When the hairs were analyzed, it was reported that they belonged to no known animal.

There were three American expeditions in 1957, 1958, and 1959, financed and led by Texas oilman Tom Slick and F. Kirk Johnson. The searchers took hypodermic rifles along to put the Yetis to sleep, but they stayed away. The men were able to get some plaster casts of footprints.

Another sighting, however, occurred in 1958. A. G. Pronin, a hydrologist at Leningrad University in the Soviet Union, sighted a Yeti in the Pamir Mountains in Central Asia. In his report he noted:

> At first glance I took it to be a bear. But then I saw it more clearly, and realized that it was a manlike creature. It was walking on two feet, upright, but in a stooping fashion. It was quite naked, and its thickset body was covered with reddish hair. The arms were overlong and swung slightly

A typical Yeti scalp preserved in a monastery at the foot of Mount Everest in the Himalayas. The photo shows Nepal's liaison officer to mountaineering groups holding the scalp that later was examined by Sir Edmund Hillary. (WIDE WORLD PHOTOS)

with each movement. I watched it for about ten minutes before it disappeared, very swiftly, among the scrub and boulders.

Because of this story, Dr. Boris Porshnev, a professor of historical science at the university in Leningrad, was appointed head of a "Commission for Studying the Abominable Snowman." He came to believe in the Yeti, saying: "In the fifteenth century, such wild people lived in the mountain vastnesses near the Gobi Desert. They had no permanent homes. Their bodies, except for hands and faces, were covered with hair. Like animals they fed on leaves, grass, and anything they could find."

Another Russian, Professor N. Stanyukovich, went to the Pamirs in 1960. He was on an expedition with prominent zoologists, archeologists, botanists, and climbers. They spent nine months in the mountains and saw nothing. In a burst of poetic inspiration, Stanyukovich wrote: "Farewell, you fascinating riddle. Farewell, inscrutable Snowman, ruler of the heights and snows. A pity, a thousand pities that you are not to be found. What, not at all? Not anywhere? Perhaps you are yet to be found in the remotest mountains of Nepal. Perhaps!"

Sir Edmund Hillary led an expedition to find the Yeti in 1960-1961. But he came back with nothing except a scalp, supposedly a Yeti's, sent to him from the Khumjung Monastery. Unfortunately, zoologists looked at the scalp and classified it as coming from a serow—a goat antelope.

In 1970, Don Whillans, the second in command of the British Annapurna Expedition, photographed footprints in the Machapuchare region of Nepal. He also said that he had seen a creature "bounding along on all fours." But that was by moonlight.

On December 14, 1972, four men left their base camp in northeastern Nepal and started on an expedition up the Kongmaa La Mountain. The four men were two Americans—Edward W. Cronin, Jr., a zoologist, Dr. Howard Emery, a physician—and two Sherpa guides.

The two Americans enjoyed the first few days of their journey, but when they reached an altitude of about 10,000 feet, they encountered a storm that filled their eyes, ears, and nostrils with snow dust. Their guides found a campsite in a valley at about 12,000 feet.

The weather was fine on that December 17, and they pitched their tents and fell asleep. During the night they had a visitor. The next morning Emery was the first up, and when he saw the footprints, he let out a shout. The prints were nine inches long and almost five inches wide.

Emery and Cronin took photographs and later made plaster casts of the tracks. Then they followed the prints until they lost the trail in the bare rocks. Cronin was sure that the footprints had not been made by "any known, normal mammal."

But the Sherpas had no doubts that it was a Yeti.

Cronin matched his own footprints made on the night of December 17 with those he made the next morning. That made him believe that all the prints near the camp had remained unaltered by the wind or the sun. He then wrote in his report:

> During the expedition we devoted special efforts to examining all large mammal prints made in snow.
>
> We noted possible variations produced by different snow conditions, terrain, and activities of the animal (*i.e.*, running, walking, etc.); a photographic record was made. We feel we can eliminate any possibility that the prints are referable to a local animal. . . .
>
> Based on this experience, I believe there is a creature alive today in the Himalayas which is creating a valid zoological mystery. . . . The evidence points to a new form of bipedal primate.

Of course there were those who disagreed. One notable scientist who had visited the Himalayas discovered that the sun could melt known animal tracks into a shape that resembled the many photographs and plaster casts of what were said to be snowman tracks. "The Yeti does not exist," he wrote. He also doubted the reliability of the observers:

> They may be excellent mountain climbers, but how qualified are they to examine spoor or interpret visual sightings? Were they tired or in some way affected by the high altitude? . . . Large unidentifiable footprints could belong to almost any of the wild animals that live in the Himalaya range. At certain gaits, bears place the hind foot partly over the imprint of the forefoot. This makes a very large imprint that looks as if it might be the print of a monster. . . . The Himalayan langur, a monkey with a long tail, often leaves prints that might be mistaken for those of a large unknown animal. . . . Markings thought to be left by the Abominable Snowman could very well have been caused by stones or lumps of snow falling from higher regions and bouncing across the slopes.

In 1978, it was reported by the Soviet news agency Tass that a Yetilike creature had been seen in Siberia. It was called *Chuchunaa* by the natives, which means "fugitive" or "outcast" in the local dialect, and was sighted in the Verkhoyansk region, 300 miles north of Yakutsk. It appeared to be six and one-half feet tall, was thin, had long arms, and was quite shaggy.

According to their report: "He feeds on raw meat and wears a reindeer skin. He cannot speak but utters shrill screams. Reindeer breeders, hunters, mushroom and berry collectors ran into him most frequently at dawn or late in the evening."

Eyewitnesses described the creature's face as human in

size, but very dark with a small forehead that protruded over the eyes like a peaked cap. Its chin was big and broad. Even though he supposedly would sneak up on houses to steal food, he would run when a human being confronted him.

Another sighting of an Abominable Snowman occurred in 1979. This report came from a British climbing team in the Himalayan Mountains. They also heard a piercing scream that sounded as if it came from a creature only a few hundred yards away.

John White, the expedition's leader, discovered several footprints that appeared to have been made by "a parent and its young." The tracks were eight inches by four inches and showed the impressions of four toes plus a thumb. They were sunk three to four inches in the snow, indicating that the creature walked upright and weighed approximately 160 pounds.

John Edwards, a squadron leader in the Royal Air Force and the lead climber, told of his sighting: "It seemed as if the creature jumped from the rocks, bounded through the snow and across a stony outcrop where the prints disappeared."

China may have an Abominable Snowman, too. Anthropologist Zhou Guoxing of the Peking Museum of Natural History announced in 1980 that there is a good reason to believe in this beast. In 1976, after sightings of a hairy biped were reported in the thickly forested, mountainous Shennongjia region, the Chinese Academy of Sciences organized a 110-member expedition, and Zhou was the scientific director.

For eight months the group collected samples of body wastes and hair and found many large footprints. They even met a creature once, but scared it off when a jumpy soldier shot himself in the leg. Analysis of the samples, according to Zhou, proved that the creature, described as six and one-half feet tall and covered with wavy, red hair, is neither man nor bear.

Regardless of what the Europeans and the Americans say, the natives of the Himalayas seem to lean toward belief in the Yeti. Naughty Tibetan children are warned about the Yeti. But they probably know the old legend that all you have to do to escape the Abominable Snowman is to run downhill. If the beast chases you, its long hair falls over its eyes and makes it blind.

But suppose you can't run downhill? Suppose the Yeti comes at you on level ground? Just pick up as many rocks and sticks as you can. Throw them one by one to the snowman. It will catch them like a major leaguer, but it won't want to put them down. Soon both of its arms are full of rocks and sticks, and you can run away.

The people of Nepal and Tibet would never think of harming a Yeti. To do so would bring bad luck and many misfortunes. Indeed, Yeti scalps, as mentioned before, are treasured in Tibetan monasteries. But there are those who say that the scalps are really made from the skin of the mountain goat.

King Mahendra of Nepal was questioned about his belief in the Yeti in 1960. His answer was given through an interpreter: "His Majesty is no expert, no anthropologist or zoologist, so he cannot say anything definite about this creature. But all the same, it pays us to keep the mystery alive."

And keep it alive they did. In 1961, the Nepalese government claimed that there really was such a creature as the Yeti, and it could be found in an S-shaped curve that included parts of Siberia, southeastern Russia, India, Alaska, Canada, and the northwestern parts of the United States.

Apparently, they wanted to make a little money out of this decision, so they granted licenses to hunt the beast in the Himalayas at $10,000 each.

In the neighboring country of Bhutan, the post office has issued triangular Yeti stamps. And the Abominable Snowman has been named the national animal of Bhutan.

But what do believing scientists have to say about the creature? In 1972, three zoologists set out to hunt the Yeti, thinking that it might be a descendant of a giant ape—*Gigantopithecus*. This is a large primate whose remains have been found both in southern China and in the Himalayas. It probably lived in the mountains of southern Asia as long ago as 9 million years and as recently as 500,000 years. There are two theories about this ape. One of them states that they were forced by the ancestors of modern man into the remote areas of the Himalayas where they might exist today, although they have become extinct in the more populated parts of the world. The other theory says that, as the mountains rose over the long ages, *Gigantopithecus* may have become isolated.

There are people who say that the Yeti is a descendant of the Neanderthal man, and is hiding out from the rest of

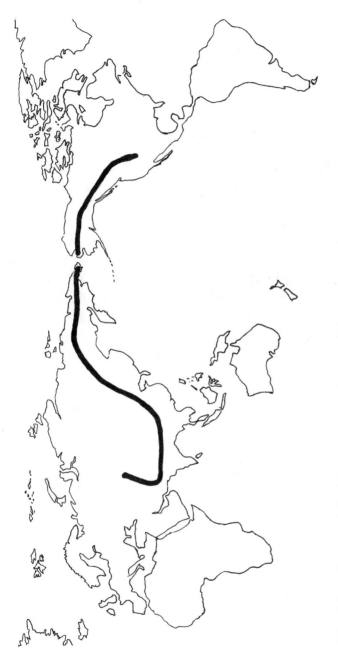

The S-shaped curve of the area in which sightings of the Yeti and Bigfoot have occurred. (VIRGINIA AYLES-WORTH)

us who are descended from the Cro-Magnon man. Still others say that it is a half-man, or hominid, who evolved separately from *Homo sapiens,* or modern man.

Some scientists dismiss the natives' belief in the Abominable Snowman as myths that are told to children to keep them in line. But perhaps they should not discard the belief. The natives are not scientifically inclined, but they do know the local wildlife, and should know the difference between a Yeti and a bear or monkey.

The vast forests of the Himalayas can support a wide variety of animals because of their rich quantities of edible plants. Not many humans live in these forests. There certainly is a possibility that many unclassified animals live in remote areas. Why not the Abominable Snowman?

Humans seem to have a need to believe in the existence of such creatures. They stimulate our curiosity. As Angus Hall once wrote:

> Perhaps this is the function that the Yeti serves for most of us. We need creatures to inhabit that strange borderland between fact and fantasy, and our interest lies not so much in whether they really exist, but in the possibility that they may exist. It is as if the very uncertainty, the remoteness, and the scanty evidence on which our ideas are based, increases the hold on us, and gives life an extra dimension it would lose if final proof came. These large creatures hovering between man and ape, grappling with nature to survive, satisfy a psychological need for many of us—just as dragons and mermaids did for our ancestors.

BIGFOOT

THE creature called Bigfoot in the United States and Sasquatch in Canada may be North America's answer to the Yeti. These beasts are said to be hairy, they walk on two feet, and they resemble human beings. They are mentioned in the folklore of the Indians of the Yukon Territory and British Columbia in Canada, the people in the northwestern United States, the Yaqui Indians of Mexico, and the Chorti Indians of Guatemala. They are considered the guardians of the wilderness.

Dr. John Napier, the curator of the primate collection of the Smithsonian Institution, said in 1973:

> Although in the last twenty years there has been a tremendous revival of public interest since these creatures have

come to the attention of "the white settlers", it is a reasonable assumption, from what we know of early written records that, like Peyton Place, the story of Sasquatch has been continuing for a great many years.

The term Sasquatch comes from an Indian word meaning "hairy giant." This beast is usually described as being from seven to nine feet tall and weighing from 600 to 900 pounds, according to sightings and analyses of plaster footprints. It is an apelike creature with thick fur, long arms, and powerful shoulders. It walks upright and its footprints measure approximately sixteen inches long and six inches wide. Most stories say that it is not ferocious.

Most reports of sightings come from a well-defined area that covers the mountains of southern British Columbia and the Cascade ranges of Washington, western Oregon, and northern California—areas of impenetrable forests. These are also areas that fit into the S-shaped curve of the habitat of the Yeti as described by the government of Nepal. The Sasquatch/Bigfoot might be a close relative of the Yeti/Abominable Snowman.

Many legends say that Bigfoot has metal fingernails and reversed feet. The latter sounds like the Yeti legends. If you meet one, it is said, it means sickness or death.

Pierre Berton writes about the myths of the Canadian Indians. The following excerpt describes their conceptions of the Bigfoot/Sasquatch creatures.

The Mahoni, who flit through the Peel River country in the northern Yukon, are enormous hairy giants with red eyes, who eat human flesh and devour entire birch trees at a gulp. The predatory Sasquatches of British Columbia's mountain caves are eight feet tall and covered with black woolly hair from head to foot. There are others, all kin to these: the terrible Brush Man of the Loucheaux in the upper Mackenzie, with his black face and yellow eyes, preying on women and children; the Weetigo of the Barrens, that horrible naked cannibal, his face black with frostbite, his lips eaten away to expose his fanglike teeth; the eight-foot, head-hunting "Mountain Men" of the Nahanni and those imaginary beings of Great Slave Lake whom the Dogrib Indians simply call "The Enemy" and fear so greatly that they must always build their homes on islands safe from the shoreline where The Enemy roam.

The first sighting of a Sasquatch track by a white man probably occurred in 1811 near what is now Jasper, Alberta, Canada. David Thompson, an explorer and trader, found a set of strange footprints in the snow. They measured fourteen inches long and eight inches wide. They also had four toes. Thompson reckoned that they could not have been the footprints of a bear, since bears have five toes.

Then, in 1844, the *Daily Colonist* of Victoria, British Columbia told of the capture of a Sasquatch. It had been seen by a train crew traveling along the Fraser River between Lytton and Yale, British Columbia. The train was stopped, and the crew chased the creature. They had to scramble up rocky hills to get the agile beast, whom they named Jacko.

According to the article, Jacko was:

> . . . Something of the gorilla type, standing about four feet
> seven inches in height and weighing 127 pounds. He has
> long black, strong hair and resembles a human being with
> one exception, his entire body, excepting his hands (or
> paws) and feet are covered with glossy hair about one inch
> long. His forearm is much longer than a man's forearm and
> he possesses extraordinary strength, as he will take hold of a
> stick and break it by wrenching it or twisting it, which no
> man living could break in the same way.

Although the rest of the story cannot be confirmed, it
was said that Jacko was put on exhibition at Yale. It became quite tame and affectionate with its keeper, who
thought of taking Jacko to London for exhibition. There
was also a rumor that the beast was later sold to the
Barnum and Bailey Circus.

The earliest written account of a Bigfoot sighting in the
United States comes from a historical pamphlet dated January 2, 1886 about Siskiyou County, California. The creature was called a "wild man," and was described in this
way: "The thing was of a gigantic size—about seven feet
high—with a bulldog head, short ears and long hair; it was
also furnished with a beard, and was free from hair on such
parts of its body as is common among men."

In 1910, two prospecting brothers named McLeod were
looking for ore in the Nahanni Valley in the northwest
territories of Canada. When they did not return to civilization on schedule, a search party went out to find them.
They found their bodies, but their heads had been cut off.
Sasquatches were blamed for the killings, and the name of

the area was changed from the Nahanni Valley to Headless Valley.

In 1917, Bigfoot struck again. A prospector's shack near Mount St. Lawrence, Washington was attacked. The *Seattle Times* printed a most lurid and imaginative story, saying: "The culprits were about eight feet tall, and were half-human, half-monster." They were also described as being able to hypnotize people, to use ventriloquism, and to make themselves invisible.

Albert Ostman, a Canadian lumberjack, claimed he had an interesting experience in 1924. He had been prospecting in a remote spot named Toba Inlet opposite Vancouver Island, and was kept prisoner for more than a week in a remote valley before he was able to escape.

The strange part of his claim was that his abductors were members of a family—mother, father, teenage son, and young daughter—all of them "near-human, hairy beasts." He had gone to sleep, and the next thing he knew, his sleeping bag, with him in it, had been picked up. After a long journey, he was dropped on the ground and he crawled out of the bag.

The creatures did not bother Ostman and even let him make his own meals from his store of food. The family turned out to be vegetarians, eating grass, roots, and spruce tips. The mother and son did the chores, bringing food back to the family. The father and daughter guarded Ostman. Not surprisingly, Ostman did not tell anyone of his adventure until 1957, fearing that he would not be believed.

Many of the people who talked to Ostman said that he

appeared to be absolutely sincere about his story. And John Napier, a professional biologist, wrote: "Ostman's description hangs together and seems to describe giant, hairy members of our own species."

The problem with Ostman's story was the part about the Sasquatches being vegetarians. The whole family put together must have weighed more than 2,000 pounds. This is the same as five male gorillas or fourteen adult humans. An expert described their food as being the poorest quality of low-energy food and the least quantity of high-energy food of any forest-type animal on earth. How could they stay alive on such a low-calorie diet?

Another wild encounter took place near Mount St. Helens in Washington State in a place that was later named Ape Canyon. This also happened in 1924.

A group of coal miners was attacked by a gang of Bigfoot creatures. The stories of how the fight started are a bit confused. One version has it that the miners saw a big apelike creature staring at them, and one of the miners grabbed a rifle and fired at it, wounding it in the head. Fred Beck, a miner, also shot another creature in the back, but its body fell over a cliff and never was found.

Another version has it that Beck was alone when he met a Bigfoot. He shot it in the back three times, killing it.

At any rate, the story goes that the friends of the Bigfoot got together and started an attack on the miners' cabin. John Napier wrote about Fred Beck's version of the battle:

> At night the apes counterattacked, opening the assault by knocking a heavy strip of wood out from between two

logs of the miners' cabin. After that there were assorted poundings on the walls, door, and roof, but the building was designed to withstand heavy mountain snows and the apes failed to break in. . . . There was . . . the sound of rocks hitting the roof and rolling off, and [the miners] did brace the heavy door from the inside.

They heard creatures thumping around on top of the cabin as well as battering the walls, and they fired shots through the walls and roof without driving them away. The noise went on from shortly after dark until near dawn. . . . The cabin had no windows and of course no one opened the door, so in fact the men inside did not see what was causing the commotion outside.

Nor could Mr. Beck say for sure . . . that there were more than two creatures outside. There were that many because there had been one on the roof and one pounding the wall simultaneously. However many there were, it was enough for the miners, who packed up and abandoned their mine the next day.

It seems that 1924 was a popular year for Bigfoot sightings. That year, a grizzled, old prospector who lived on the east slope of Mount St. Helens left his cabin in search of a forest ranger. When he found a ranger, he told this tale:

They woke me up in the middle of the night, throwin' stones at my place. Some of them stones was big ones, some even come through the roof. And all the time they was around the house, they was screaming like a bunch of apes. I didn't dare go outside. That's probably what they wanted me to do. Would you have gone outside? No sir! Instead I crawled under the bed, and I stayed there till morning come. Sometime in the night them critters quit their screamin' and slunk off in the dark. Next morning when I went outside there was the tracks, big ones, a foot or more across, and right up beside my place.

Several people claimed to have sighted a Bigfoot near Yankton, Oregon, in 1926. A truck driver swore that one of them had trotted along beside his logging truck, looking into the cab at him.

Another Bigfoot attack supposedly occurred on a Nevada farm in 1940. While the creature banged on the front of the house, the farmer's wife ran out the back, taking her children with her. When she came back, she found huge footprints around the house.

In 1941, Mrs. George Chapman, who lived near Blaine, Washington, reported another sighting. She said that she and her children saw "an eight-foot hairy man come out of the woods." The creature entered a lean-to behind her cabin, and Mrs. Chapman and her children went out the front door. They hid in the forest for a long time, and when they finally returned to the cabin, they found huge tracks.

A deputy sheriff from Blaine made casts of the footprints, and they appeared to be the largest Bigfoot prints of all time, measuring sixteen inches in length. Unfortunately, the beast had tramped down the Chapmans' potato patch as it went back into the forest.

William Roe met a Sasquatch in 1955 in a place called Tete Jaune Cache in British Columbia. In his sworn statement, he said:

My first impression was of a huge man about six feet tall, almost three feet wide, and probably weighing somewhere near 300 pounds. It was covered from head to foot with dark brown, silver-tipped hair . . . the hair that covered it, leaving bare only the parts of its face around the mouth, nose, and ears, made it resemble an animal as much as a human. None of this hair, even on the back of its head, was longer than an inch.

A breakthrough in Bigfoot sightings happened in 1967. On October 20, Roger Patterson and his friend Bob Gimlin were high in the mountains of northern California. According to Patterson's story, ". . . when riding horseback up a creek bottom, we encountered this creature. My horse smelled it, jumped, and fell. I got the camera out of the saddlebag and ran across the creek and we were able to get twenty-nine feet of sixteen millimeter colored film."

They tracked Bigfoot's trail for three miles before they lost it in the undergrowth. But they did make plaster casts of the fourteen-and-one-half-inch prints.

The film was developed and sent to Hollywood, where experts in movie special effects studied it. These men, who knew every trick about faking motion pictures, decided that the footage was genuine.

The film was then shown to scientists, many of whom were zoologists. Some of them commented on the rather odd and exaggerated walk that the creature seemed to have. They claimed that it looked like a bad actor trying to imitate the walk of a monster. Others commented on the movement of the muscles as the Bigfoot walked. They felt that this movement was proof enough that the creature was real and the Patterson movie authentic.

Patterson's film showed what appeared to be a female Bigfoot. She was walking upright like a human being, and she appeared to be about seven and one-half feet tall, and three feet across the shoulders. She had arms three feet long, and it was estimated that she must have weighed about 800 pounds.

John Napier, one of the scientists, remained a bit skeptical, although he admitted that there was nothing in the film that proved conclusively that it was a hoax. "In effect, what I mean was that I could not see the zipper, and I still can't," he said.

Some of the most persuasive evidence for the existence of Bigfoot, according to Napier, was a set of footprints found near Bossburg, Washington, in 1969. There were 1,089 of them and the trail extended for a half-mile. The right footprints seemed to have been made by a crippled foot. The prints looked human except for the fact that they were seventeen and one-half inches long and seven inches wide.

Napier said: "They are not the footprints of modern man, but could conceivably be the footprints of unknown members of the human family."

He also felt that they were not fake footprints. "It is very difficult to conceive of a hoaxer so subtle, so knowledgeable, and so sick as to fake a footprint of this nature," he said.

In 1970, another Bigfoot film appeared on the scene. But unlike Patterson's, this was clearly a fake. The film was

A frame from the Patterson movie. (WIDE WORLD PHOTOS)

supposed to have been shot at one place, but the creature was filmed walking past a distinctive, dwarf apple tree that people who knew the region recognized as being in a very different place. Additionally, a month before the film was taken, the photographer was seen buying an old fur coat in a Goodwill Industries store. Blowups of some of the frames of the film showed stitching at the joints of the creature.

In 1974, the American Yeti Expedition included a number of respected scientists and was financed by a grant administered by the National Wildlife Federation. The expedition tracked a creature near Mount St. Helens, Washington that went up a small stream for about twenty yards and then circled above the trackers. It seemed to want to observe them, instead of the opposite.

A sample of hair from the creature was identified as human and possibly from an ankle or a leg. Mary Joe Florey, a microbiologist from Portland, Oregon said: "I'm not saying it was a Bigfoot, but it's very unlikely a barefooted human would be running around in that area. And if it was a human, why would it want to hide from other humans?"

The hairs were found on fresh "scuff marks" on a moss-covered rock. Huge, humanlike tracks were found in an area where deer and cattle had been killed "by something very large." Robert W. Morgan, the leader of the expedition, reported finding "the longest string of Bigfoot tracks ever examined by scientists to my knowledge. Field measurements indicated the footprints were a whopping eighteen inches long, seven inches across the ball of the foot, and five and one-half inches across the heel. The average stride was well over fifty inches."

Another scientist, Professor Grover Krantz, a physical anthropologist from Washington State University, said that the creature that made the tracks must have been more than eight feet tall and in the 800-pound range. He commented: "It is overwhelmingly probable that the tracks are real. I've seen some mighty sophisticated fakes. I don't think these could have been done with fake feet."

In 1974, Jean Fitzgerald, a woman who lives near Roseburg, Oregon, claimed that she had been watching a Bigfoot in the Umpqua National Forest near her home. This monster would make daily trips to the lake to catch frogs. Ms. Fitzgerald explained: "You might think I'm crazy, but it seems very intelligent. It hasn't threatened us yet and it has a raven that always accompanies it. The bird talks to the monster and almost seems like a pet."

In the fall of 1975, more than one hundred reports of Bigfoot sightings came from the Lummi Indian Reservation seven miles west of Bellingham, Washington. And in October 1975, a Canadian trapper claimed to have seen a family of Sasquatches. Bob Moody was working in the Woking area, 230 miles northwest of Edmonton, Alberta, when he spotted the creatures from his truck.

"I'm an old bushman," he said. "There's no way they were bears." Moody said he had seen an adult Sasquatch traveling on the edge of Highway 2 with two young ones. The Royal Canadian Mounted Police said that they were not going to involve themselves in an investigation.

In 1976, the army corps of engineers officially recognized

A resident of Sussex County, New Jersey holds a plaster cast of a footprint found in the area where several farmers reported seeing a hairy, humanlike creature in the summer of 1976. (WIDE WORLD PHOTOS)

the Bigfoot in its *Washington Environmental Atlas.* It was described as standing up to twelve feet tall and weighing as much as 1,000 pounds. But the *Atlas* admitted that the existence of Bigfoot is "hotly disputed."

Between September and November 1977, there were twenty-eight sightings of a Bigfoot near Little Eagle, South Dakota. Most of the residents of the town were Sioux Indians. The Reverend Angus Long Elk decided to leave the area until the fuss died down. He said: "I couldn't stand its running around and shrieking all night. It was doing it all the time and about two weeks ago my

wife saw it at night while she was down by the river. She's
been afraid ever since and wants to leave."

Leonce Boudreaux of Krotz Springs, Louisiana claims
that he twice saw a 500-pound hairy Bigfoot in the woods
near his home. The first sighting was in October 1977 and
the second in June 1978. The first time, he was afraid that
people would laugh at him so he kept the incident a se-
cret. The second time, however, he did tell his story. "The
only reason I did report it is because I felt like I had
enough evidence to prove there was something there," he
said.

He and his brother-in-law had found a place in the
woods where something was bedding down, but wildlife
agents would only admit that some large animal was making a bed there. Captain Winton Vidrine of the state wildlife and fisheries division said: "I really believe it is a bear
complaint. I don't believe in Bigfoot."

The Sioux Indians once believed in Bigfoot, calling him
Taku he, and felt that something awful would happen to
their tribes if he were hunted or hurt. In 1978, Pat Mc-
Laughlin, the tribal chairman of the Standing Rock Sioux
tribe, published a legal notice in the Mobridge (South Dakota) *Tribune*: "We will authorize NO search initiated or
participated in by employees of any tribal program or the
Bureau of Indian Affairs, day or night, nor will any out-
siders be allowed to hunt Bigfoot on this reservation."

Bigfoot and Sasquatch are believed to be relatives of the
Yeti. Reports indicate they have been sighted in the
S-shaped area of the world mentioned before. The Cheha-
lis Indians of British Columbia think that Sasquatch is

OH ...AH (BIGFOOT)

The redwood statue of Bigfoot on display at Willow Creek, California. (WILLOW CREEK CHAMBER OF COMMERCE)

descended from two bands of giants that were destroyed in a battle many years ago. The Kwakiutl Indians of British Columbia have a Sasquatch on their totem poles. And in Skamania County, Washington, the county commissioners passed a law making anyone who kills a Bigfoot subject to a fine of $1,000 and five years in jail. In the last ten years, there have been more than 300 registered sightings of Bigfoot and Sasquatch, but none of the creatures has been captured.

With all these reports of sightings, plus Patterson's film, the supposed evidence of the existence of Sasquatch and Bigfoot should not be taken lightly. There is so much interest in these creatures that organizations have been set up to seek them out.

Before his death in 1972, Roger Patterson headed the Northwest Research Association. This group mapped out a complete course of action to capture a Bigfoot. Patterson explained: "When a specimen is obtained, all personnel and equipment will be concentrated on it." He expected to shoot the creature with drug-carrying darts and then keep it under sedation for as long as the examination lasted.

All field forces would be rushed to the scene, and a call would go out for a helicopter to transport Bigfoot to the examination place. Blood, bone marrow, and body fluid samples would be collected and analyzed. Plaster casts would be made of teeth, jaws, hands, and feet.

The whole procedure would be photographed and tape recorded. Security measures would go into effect at once. One reason would be to protect the scientists against an attack by other Bigfoot creatures. The other reason, as Patterson explained, would be the need "to protect the field group against interference by everybody, including the press."

In 1973, the American Wildlife Research Organization announced that it was being computerized. They were going to study the 600 Bigfoot sightings that had been reported over the last fourteen years. The director of the project, Ronald Olsen, hoped that the computer would reveal patterns of behavior and habitat that might give more information about the creature.

One of the centers of Bigfoot activity is around the county-seat town of The Dalles, Oregon. According to their sheriff's office, five people testified that they had seen the creature in the area on June 2, 1971. That appears to be a one-day record for sightings.

The Dalles was also the site of the Bigfoot Information Center. The center was run by Peter Byrne, who was formerly a professional hunter in Nepal and searched for the Yeti. Then he decided to concentrate on the Bigfoot. The center investigated each reported sighting and used a network of volunteer investigators.

Byrne believed that he collected the details of over ninety-four sightings that are believable. The center was supported by admission fees to a small exhibit and donations from other sources, including the Academy of Applied Science, which was one of the chief supporters of another enterprise—the search for the Loch Ness Monster. But in 1980, Byrne decided to stop his investigations. He had not been able to prove the existence of Bigfoot.

Perhaps there is no such thing as Bigfoot or Sasquatch. But as George Laycock, an eminent naturalist, said:

> Bigfoot will almost certainly appear again. People all the way over into Montana and Wyoming, and other states as well, talk of the Bigfoot. Many would not be at all surprised to find these shaggy giants living in their mountains, too. Doubters sometime suggest that anyone with a mountain and a forest can have his own Sasquatch.
>
> One thing is certain. If Bigfoot is really out there in the hills, his name belongs on the government's official list of rare and endangered species. Whatever his fortunes might have been in the past, his numbers have dwindled to a precious few.

3 OTHER CREATURES ON THE LAND

IN addition to those who claim to have seen the Yeti/ Abominable Snowman or the Bigfoot/Sasquatch, the world seems to be filled with people who have reported the sightings of other kinds of monsters. In the forests of Indonesia, there is supposed to be a manlike monster called the *Orang Pendek*, for example. Some of the Indians of Quebec tell of the Windigo, a huge, manlike creature that goes naked in the bush and eats Indians. The Windigo makes a sinister hissing noise and occasionally lets out fearful howls. This strikes terror in the hearts of those who hear it.

There are also many people who claim to have seen animal-like monsters. In 1919, a Monsieur Lepage was in charge of railroad construction in the Belgian Congo. One day, when he was out in the jungle, he came across a fierce creature. The animal, he said, "was some twenty-four feet in length with a long pointed snout adorned with tusks like horns and a short horn above the nostrils. The front feet were like those of a horse, and the hind hooves were cloven."

He claimed that later the beast rampaged through a native village and killed some of the inhabitants. The Belgian government promptly forbade anyone hurting or molesting the animal.

Then there was the giant kangaroo that was seen by the Reverend W. J. Hancock of South Pittsburgh, Tennessee. In January 1934, Hancock described what he saw: "It was as fast as lightning and looked like a giant kangaroo run-

Some people will believe in anything. This is an old etching of a monster that was supposedly seen in Chile. It consists of parts of a number of different animals.

ning and leaping across the field." He said that the beast had just killed and eaten a large dog. The owner of the dog also saw the creature and agreed with the description. As other dogs disappeared, and then chickens were missing, the giant kangaroo was blamed, but it was never found.

There have been creatures resembling Bigfoot seen far away from the northwestern states. Several have been reported in the Midwest. Unlike his western cousins, the Michigan Bigfoot has been known to be violent and dangerous. There is a place near Charlotte, Michigan that is said to be called Gorilla Swamp because of a hairy creature that lives there.

In 1965, there was a sighting in Wisconsin. A hairy monster was said to have reached through the window of a car and grabbed one of the two women riding in the automobile. He grabbed her by the hair and the other woman later told of the attack: "We both screamed, but the monster kept beating her head against the door until Christine fainted. I jumped out of the car and ran to a house for help." The creature was never caught, but in September 1965, a month later, four teenagers reported to the police in Decatur, Illinois that their car had been approached by a large, hairy, manlike monster.

This item appeared in an issue of the *Union Banner* of Clanton, Alabama in 1965—obviously a great year for monster sightings:

> Some six years ago several people out on Walnut Creek a mile or so from Clanton reported seeing some kind of animal like a bear. It made some curious sounds at night

kindly [sic] like a woman in distress. It ranged up and down the creek for a distance of some ten miles.

Then some four years ago something made tracks in peach orchards some three miles south of Clanton, near large swamps. It was supposed to vanish into the swamps at night. A cement cast was made of the track, about the size of a person's foot, but looking more like a hand. The cast is still somewhere in Clanton.

Perhaps one of the strangest creatures ever sighted was the Minnesota Iceman. The beast was described as being hairy and humanlike, and it had supposedly been owned by a mysterious West Coast millionaire.

Beginning in 1967, the iceman was exhibited at carnivals and fairs, mostly in the Midwest. The creature was frozen in a block of ice and sealed in a refrigerated, glass case—hence its name. Frank Hansen, a carnival showman, was the exhibitor, and he claimed that it was a "man left over from the Ice Age," and that the body had been found frozen in a 6,000-pound block of ice found in the Bering Strait. Hansen charged his customers twenty-five cents per look. He traveled with it for eighteen months, and when the carnival season was over in the winter of 1968, he took the iceman to his farm near Winona, Minnesota.

Just by chance, two men heard of the whereabouts of the Minnesota Iceman. One of them was Ivan Sanderson, a science writer and a part-time monster buff. The other was his houseguest Bernard Heuvelmans, a Belgian naturalist, who had written a book on unknown animals and one on sea serpents. Off they went to Hansen's farm to have a look at the body.

They found it encased in a block of ice and stored in a refrigerated coffin. One of the first things they noticed was that the iceman had apparently been shot. Its right eye had been hit by a bullet and the back of his skull had been shattered. That did away with the story that it had been frozen in the ice for centuries. Hansen admitted that he thought the monster had been murdered.

Their examination lasted for two days, and it was not too successful. To begin with, the coffin was stored in a small, poorly lit trailer, and making sketches of the creature was difficult. In order to make drawings, Sanderson had to lie on top of the plate-glass lid of the coffin with his nose almost touching the iceman's nose. They also took photographs, and Heuvelmans wrote a paper for the Royal Institute of Natural Sciences in Belguim, which he called, "Preliminary Note on a Specimen Preserved in Ice; An Unknown Living Hominid." The two men had obviously accepted the iceman as a real specimen and had believed Hansen's story about the murder.

Heuvelmans wrote: "The specimen at first sight is representative of man . . . of fairly normal proportions, but excessively hairy . . . His skin is of the waxlike color of corpses of men . . . when not tanned by the sun. . . ."

Then the plot thickened. In the beginning, Hansen had exhibited the iceman, billing it as the Siberkoye Creature and claiming that it had been frozen since the Ice Age. Then, when the bullet wound had been found, he claimed that he had shot the creature himself. Story number three appeared in a national tabloid, the *National Bulletin*. Helen Westring claimed that she had been attacked by the Minnesota Iceman in 1966 while she was on a hunting trip near Bemidji, Minnesota. She said that it had hypnotized her with its pink eyes, she fainted, it attacked her, and when she regained consciousness, she shot it through the right eye.

In 1969, the iceman returned to the carnival circuit billed as a "creature frozen and preserved forever in a coffin of ice." But there was something different about it. Hansen admitted that he was now exhibiting a latex replica of the original.

Meanwhile, Sanderson approached Dr. John Napier to see if he might be interested in scientifically examining the beast. Napier was quite interested until he heard from S. Dillon Ripley, the secretary of the Smithsonian Institution. Ripley had not only found out that the iceman was now just a model, but also, since the murder theory was now known, he had asked the Federal Bureau of Investigation to trace the original iceman. The head of the FBI at the time, J. Edgar Hoover, rejected the idea and pointed out that there was no apparent violation of federal law in the killing of a nonhuman. Hansen immediately prepared a new display sign for the iceman: "The near-Man . . . Investigated by the FBI."

The hoax was discovered when the public relations office of the Smithsonian turned up a commercial model-making organization on the West Coast which claimed that it had constructed the original iceman model in 1967, just before it went on the carnival circuit. Needless to say, both Napier and the Smithsonian decided not to investigate the Minnesota Iceman further.

Another strange creature was seen near El Reno, Oklahoma in 1970. It was the Abominable Chickenman, and was said to walk like a gorilla, leave manlike handprints, rip doors off their hinges, and steal chickens.

A rancher was checking his chicken house one day when he found the door torn from its hinges. Also, some of his chickens were missing. Handprints and footprints were all over the coop. He became suspicious that this was not a normal chicken thief when he realized that the creature was walking around without shoes in the month of December.

The prints were examined by many people. The director of the Oklahoma City Zoo was quoted as saying that the prints looked to him like those of an animal that walked on both its hands and feet such as gorillas and chimpanzees. He said: "It appears that whatever made the prints was walking on all fours."

Other chicken-house robberies complete with strange handprints and footprints were reported, but not all the people of the region were convinced. A game ranger, for example, complained: "A lot of people are having a big laugh over this. They are referring to the 'thing' as the Abominable Chickenman. But they'd cut out the wisecracks real quick if they saw some of those tracks around their homes." Fortunately, the doings of the chickenman have not been reported since early in 1971, and many Oklahomans hope it will not return.

Goatman supposedly roamed the countryside of northern Prince Georges County, Maryland for quite some time. It has even become a local legend with the high school crowd. They have been known to spray-paint walls or trees with the statement, "Goatman was here." Everytime a dog is killed mysteriously, goatman is blamed.

It is supposed to be the size of a man. It walks like a man. It has a man's face. But it is a furry creature. Some say the fur is found all over its body, others think it is found only on the lower part of the body like the satyrs in Greek mythology.

There are some who think that goatman used to be a scientist who experimented on goats at the National Agricultural Research Center in Prince Georges County. Something went wrong with his experiments and his body became covered with hair. Naturally, looking like that, he ran away and lived in a shack in the woods. He came out every so often to kill dogs or jump on passing cars to beat them with an ax.

In July 1972, a creature made its appearance in Louisiana, Missouri. Some youngsters saw a tall, hairy, two-legged creature in a nearby woods staring intently at their house. The beast was seen several times in the next few days, and was described as being "anywhere from six to twelve feet tall, and had a terrible smell." One person swore that he had seen it crossing a highway with a sheep or dog in its mouth. Others said that it had a dog under its arm and described the thing as looking like a bear.

It didn't take long for newspaper reporters to christen the monster Mo-Mo. This was short for Missouri Monster. Soon more people were stepping forward to give evidence.

Two girls admitted that in 1971 they were on a picnic near Highway 79, north of Louisiana, when a "half-ape, half-man" came out of the woods and headed toward them. They ran to their car and leaped in, locking the doors against the intruder. Unfortunately, they couldn't drive away because they had left the car keys in their picnic basket.

One of the girls told reporters: "It walked upright on two feet and its arms dangled way down. The arms were partially covered with hair but the hands and palms were hairless. We had plenty of time to see this because the thing came right over to the car and inspected it. . . . This ape man actually tried to figure out how to open the doors."

They tried blowing the horn of the car, and that seemed to worry Mo-Mo. It left the vicinity of the automobile, but went to the laid-out lunch and ate a peanut-butter sandwich before it went back into the woods.

One of the girls defended their report. "We'd have difficulty proving that the experience occurred, but all you have to do is go into those hills to realize that an army of those things could live there undetected."

There is a town called Grahamsville in the Catskill Mountain region of New York State. In 1972, people living near the town reported seeing a monkeylike creature wandering around. Naturally, it was dubbed the Grahamsville Gorilla.

In 1973, a new monster was supposedly discovered in southern Florida. This creature appeared one night inside a drive-in movie theater near Ft. Lauderdale. A young man had wandered away from his car, and something came up from behind and hit him, knocking him unconscious.

When he recovered, he found himself staring into the fur-covered face of a giant creature. All the young man could say was, "I knew that what I saw was no human."

Other people began reporting sightings of this beast. Four students claimed to have seen it in the Everglades in broad daylight. This time, part of the report was that the thing had a horrible body odor, and the creature became known as the skunk-ape.

Another man reported that he had hit the skunk-ape with his car as the creature was crossing the road at night. The wounded monster limped off into the swamp from which it had come. Police refused to confirm that the man had indeed hit the skunk-ape.

According to other stories, the skunk-ape visited trailer courts to go through the garbage cans. It was supposed to be bigger than a man, heavy bodied, and covered with brownish fur splotched with gray. It had also been seen in the company of a baby skunk-ape. Hunts were organized, but so far the creature has not been captured.

The skunk-ape even made the national news on three television networks. That was a milestone because most monster stories get only local coverage. Walter Cronkite didn't seem too impressed, however.

In an effort to be scientific, the sighters of the creature even came up with a classification system for the skunk-ape. They say that there are two species of the creature. The larger species has three toes and is violent. The smaller has five toes and is shy and harmless.

On January 8, 1974, the skunk-ape made another visit. Richard Lee Smith reported that he had struck a huge, hairy, manlike creature on an Everglades highway. Smith said:

> It jumped out at me. I swerved to miss it and almost hit another car head-on. I thought it was a big man with no clothes on. It was hairy and looked to be seven or eight feet tall. It jumped across the guardrail right in front of me and I just couldn't avoid it. I hit it on the leg with my right fender. It didn't scream or make any sound when I hit it. I've never seen anything like it before.

Three hours later, another motorist called the highway patrol and announced that he had seen "a large seven- or eight-foot thing limping" along US Route 27, just seven miles south of the alleged accident.

Patrolman Robert Holmeyer of the Hialeah Gardens Police arrived at the scene just in time to see "a shadowy dark thing crashing off into the brush. It looked like a man, except it was an extremely large man—about eight feet. It was running, beating out a path in the saw grass."

Cary Kanter was a security guard on duty patrolling an unfinished housing project near Palm Beach, Florida late in 1974. He saw something move in the nearby bushes and trained his Jeep headlights on the thing. But the huge form moved toward him.

Kanter pulled his revolver and told it to stop. Unfortunately, it kept on coming. It was reported to be about seven feet tall and was hairy and smelly. Kanter described the aroma: "It smelled like it had taken a bath in rotten eggs. It made my nose water and my eyes fill up."

When the skunk-ape was less than thirty feet away, Kanter fired six rounds of bullets at it. "It grabbed its chest and ran like you can't believe—like a track star."

One of the strangest of all these monsters was seen bounding about in the middle of Illinois in 1973. It had pink eyes and three legs, and was seen by a Henry McDaniel in Enfield, Illinois.

He and his family were sitting in their house on April 25, when they heard a strange scratching at the door. McDaniel picked up his gun and a flashlight and went out to investigate what he thought was a case of a prowling animal. Then he saw the creature.

"It was about three feet from me," he reported. "I wasn't scared. Then I saw those pink eyes shine at me like a reflector on a car. It had pink eyes, a large head, and was kind of dirtyish-gray color . . . hairy . . . about four or five feet tall. Standing right in front of the door on three legs just like a human being."

He claimed that he had shot at the monster several times, and he also thought that he had hit it with at least one of the shots. The creature hissed at him and leaped away. McDaniel estimated that in three jumps it had cleared about seventy-five feet. It ran down a nearby railroad track and disappeared into the darkness.

The next morning McDaniel was awakened by the barking of his dog. He went to the door, looked out, and there was the monster on the railroad tracks. He said: "I wasn't scared. I'd like to have it as a pet and charge admission. It's something that's there and we've got to accept it."

The Enfield Monster was never seen again. But other

people did find strange-looking six-toed-tracks around the McDaniel house.

In the fall of 1974, the *Wall Street Journal* published a story about a phantom kangaroo, saying that it stood better than four feet tall, weighed about 125 pounds, and had either a brownish-red or a brownish-gray coat. It had been seen around the Chicago area that fall, but also must have taken side trips to Indiana, Wisconsin, and southern Illinois. It had been sighted more than fifty times.

Even President Gerald Ford got into the act when he said: "The Chicago Bears want him for their backfield, and the Democrats want to register him to vote—at least once."

The closest confrontation came when two Chicago policemen, Leonard Ciangi and Michael Byrne, swore that they saw the beast at about 3:30 A.M. on October 18, chased it down an alley, and cornered it in a fenced-in yard. The creature stood on its tail, they said, and acted defensively. Then it jumped the fence and hopped away.

Byrne said: "It started to scream and get vicious. My partner got kicked pretty bad in the legs. The kangaroo smacks pretty good, but we got in a few punches to the head and he must have felt it. Too bad we didn't have our nightsticks there. Then we could have really hammered him."

Byrne then talked about the kangaroo's escape. "If I could have caught up with him, I would have given him a speeding ticket. It was a fifteen miles per hour zone."

The morning after the confrontation, the police switchboard was swamped with complaints from people saying that the kangaroo was rummaging around in their garbage cans. And a truck driver claimed that the kangaroo bounced across the road in front of him while he was driving near Lansing, Illinois. There were also several sightings in Indiana and Wisconsin, and it had even been seen in Evanston, Illinois on the campus of Northwestern University.

Finally, a Russian report of 1976 stated that during World War II, a Soviet army patrol searching for deserters in the Caucasus captured a muscular, hairy "Man-beast." Because they didn't know what to do with it, and couldn't make themselves understood, the soldiers shot it as a deserter.

There are several explanations for all these strange stories about wondrous creatures. The first one is, obviously, that they are fakes. If one wants to make up a story about being attacked by a monster, what could be better than describing a big, hairy, manlike creature? And if one wants to dress up as a monster to fool others, it is much easier to dress up in a Yeti-type suit than as a fire-breathing dragon. For example, in the case of the Grahamsville Gorilla, the police actually found a gorilla costume in an automobile. Even an old fur coat and hat would do as a costume after dark.

Another explanation for the popularity of the hairy monster is that the belief in these creatures psychologically takes us back to the time of our ancestors. These monsters were very popular in the Middle Ages. Many people believed in a wild man who was large, strong, and hairy. He was generally thought of as a debased or fallen human being, and lived in the forest apart from civilization. He tore up trees when he was angry. He carried off women.

Professor Richard Bernheimer leans toward this explanation. He once wrote:

> It appears that the notion of the wild man must respond and be due to a persistent psychological urge. We may define this urge as the valid need to give external expression and symbolically valid form to the impulses of reckless physical self-assertion which are hidden in all of us, but are normally kept under control. These impulses, which are strongest and most aggressive in the very young, are restricted slowly, as the child learns to come to terms with a civilized environment, which will not tolerate senseless noise, wanton destruction, and uncalled for interference with its activities. But the repressed desire for such unhampered self-assertion persists and may finally be projected outward as the image of a man who is free as the beasts, able and ready to try his strength without regard for the consequences to others, and therefore be able to call up forces which his civilized brother has repressed in his effort at self-control. In contrast to civilized man, the wild man is a child of nature, upon whose hidden resources he can depend since he has not removed himself from its guidance and tutelage.

A final explanation states that these beasts really are unknown species of fearsome animals. Some believe that they are some sort of animal that was previously thought to have been extinct. Others believe that they are some form of subhuman or primitive, manlike being. After all, evolution is not a simple straight line from ape to man. Many side branches were formed and appeared to die off. Or did they?

It's difficult to imagine how a species of monster could have remained hidden for so long. But on the other hand, many new species of animals are discovered every year. True, they tend to be insignificant in our views—animals such as previously unknown mites that live in the nasal passages of birds, for example.

But it has been estimated that, even if we eliminate Antarctica, nearly one-tenth of the land surface of the earth is unexplored. There are vast areas of the United States that contain some huge wildernesses where a large creature or even a whole tribe of them could hide.

If this is hard to believe, just consider Great Britain. Our impression of the British Isles is that all of it has been thoroughly explored. This is true, of course, but there are areas which, although explored, are not frequently visited by humans. Yet even in the early 1970s, thirty years after the end of World War II, there were cases where downed military planes were found in some obscure corners of a forest.

And the fighter plane, unlike a manlike monster, obviously was not trying to hide from detection. There just are many places on the surface of the earth where a canny creature could hide from the rest of us.

CREATURES IN
THE SEA

THE sea has been a place of mystery ever since the beginning of the human race. Probably one of the earliest sea creatures on record was the fish-god of Babylonia. Its name was Ea, or Oannes, and it was described more than 4,000 years ago. Down to the waist it was a handsome man with a beard. But below the waist, it was a fish complete with scales and a tail. It was the creature that came out of the Persian Gulf to teach the Babylonians how to write and to give them lessons in the arts and sciences.

There were other fish-men described in ancient writings. The ancient Hindus, the Greeks, and the Romans all had them in their mythologies.

In the Western world, during the sixteenth century, there seemed to be a rash of fish-men and fish-women.

There is one story of a creature captured in Norway that looked like a monk. One medieval writer described it: "It had a man's face, rude and ungraceful with a bald, shining head; on the shoulders something resembling a monk's cowl; and long winglets instead of arms. The extremity of the body ended in a tail."

According to the story, the monkfish was given to the king of Poland. He then took pity on it and had it put back into the sea.

In the last part of the sixteenth century, there was an account of a sea serpent:

> . . . With seven heades that was sent out of Turkey to Venice embalmed, which long after was made a present to Francis de Valoys, the French king, by whom for the rareness of it, was valued at 6000 ducats. Nature hath never brought out a form anything more marvellous amongst the monsters that ever were, for besides the fearfull figure of this serpent, there is yet a further consideration and regarde touchying the faces, which both in view and judgement seem more human than brutal.

Stories of giant sea serpents have been around for a long time. The ancient Greek philosopher Aristotle told of a serpent that had attacked and capsized ships off the coast of Libya. The kings of ancient Delphi and Thebes believed that they were related to serpents. The first king of Athens was believed to have been half-man and half-serpent. And there were those who thought that the father of Alexander the Great was a serpent.

The Chinese had their god Foki, and the Hindus had their Krishna, both of whom are sometimes pictured as part reptile. There were places in Wales where the natives believed that men could turn into snakes.

In 1522, a strange monster that was estimated to be fifty cubits long—that is about seventy-five feet—was sighted off the coast of Norway. Archbishop Olaus Magnus of Sweden described in 1555 a sea monster two hundred feet long and twenty feet in circumference. It had a lion's mane, fiery eyes, and was covered with scales. This one could not only sink ships, but it also would appear from the depths, grab sailors off the decks of their boats, and eat them.

Then there were the stories of the Kraken. One of these beasts supposedly swam too close to the shore of Norway in 1680. It got stuck in a cleft of a rock and remained there until it died. The smell from the decaying body caused air

A sixteenth-century sea monster threatens a ship.

pollution for miles around, and it was months before the people could return to their homes.

In 1734, another Kraken was described by the Danish missionary Hans Egede. He said it was sighted near Greenland.

> The monster was of so huge a size that, coming out of the water, its head reached as high as a mainmast; its body was as bulky as the ship, and three or four times as long. It had a long pointed snout, and spouted like a whale-fish; it had great broad paws; the body seemed covered with shellwork, and the skin was very ragged and uneven. The under part of its body was shaped like an enourmous huge serpent, and when it dived again under the water, it plunged backward into the sea, and so raised its tail aloft, which seemed a whole ship's length distant from the bulkiest part of its body.

Erik Pontoppidan, the bishop of Bergen, Norway in the eighteenth century, described another Kraken. He wrote a book about the natural history of his country in 1752, and it was clear that, while he had never seen a sea monster, he believed the stories about them. He described the Kraken this way:

> Its back or upper part, which seems to be about an English mile-and-a-half in circumference, looks at first like a number of small islands surrounded by something that floats and fluctuates like seaweed . . . at last several bright points or horns appear, which grow thicker and thicker the higher they rise above the water. . . . After the monster has

An Egede's Kraken disports himself in this engraving, while another one stretches out full-length to show off his humps.

been on the surface for a short time it begins slowly to sink again, and then the danger is as great as before, because the motion of his sinking causes such a swell in the sea and such an eddy or whirlpool that it draws everything down with it.

Late in the eighteenth century, a Danish sailing ship was becalmed off the western coast of Africa. The captain, Jean-Magnus Dens, ordered the crew to go overboard to scrape and clean the hull of the ship. They worked from planks suspended over the ship's sides.

Suddenly, a sea monster appeared, grabbed two of the men, and dragged them into the sea. A third man was grabbed, but he held on to the rigging and his mates cut off one of the monster's arms. Then the creature sank below the surface. The two men were never found, and the third man died that night.

Dens described the arm as being very thick at one end and tapering to a point at the other. It was twenty-five feet long and covered with suckers. He estimated that the whole arm must have been from thirty-five to forty feet long.

Such stories were often believed in earlier times, but this one was so fantastic that few people swallowed it whole. One person who did, however, was a French naturalist, Pierre Denys de Montfort. He thought that Dens' monster was a giant octopus. He included the story in his book, *The Natural History of Molluscs,* which was a six-volume work published in Paris between 1802 and 1805. Most people made fun of his writings.

Montfort continued his studies, however, compiling reports of "the sightings of monsters and serpents of the sea by mariners whose sincerity I do not and will not doubt."

In the 1790s, he went to the port of Dunkirk, France where a group of American whaling sailors lived and worked. He interviewed these men. One of his reports stated:

> One of these captains, named Ben Johnson, told me that he had harpooned a male whale, which, . . . seemed to have [a long organ] coming out of its mouth. This surprised him greatly, and also the sailors, and when they had made the whale fast to the ship, he had them put a hook through this long round mass of flesh which they hauled in with several running nooses . . . they could hardly believe their eyes when they saw that this fleshy mass, cut off at both ends and as thick as a mast at the widest point, was the arm of an enormous octopus, the closed suckers of which were larger than a hat; the lower end seemed newly cut off, the upper one . . . was also cut off and scarred and surmounted by a sort of extension as thick and long as a man's arm.
>
> This huge octopus's limb, exactly measured with a fishing line, was found to be thirty-five feet long, and the suckers were arranged in two rows, as in the common octopus. What then must have been the length of arm which had been cut off at its upper extremity where it was no less than six inches in diameter?

Montfort thought that about ten feet had been cut off the upper end, and ten to twenty-five feet off the lower end. That made a total length of about eighty feet.

Another story that he collected was told by an American captain named Reynolds. "One day," Monfort wrote, "he and his men saw floating on the surface of the water a long fleshy body, red and slate colored, which they took to be a sea serpent, and which frightened the sailors who rowed the whale boats."

But one of the men noticed that this huge snake had no head, so it must have been dead. They hauled it on board. To them it looked like an octopus or squid arm, having suckers and measuring forty-five feet long and two and one-half feet in diameter.

Another story recorded by Montfort concerned a sailing ship from St. Malo. It was off the coast of western Africa when it was attacked by a "monster straight from Hell." According to Montfort:

> The ship had just taken in her cargo of slaves, ivory, and gold dust, and the men were heaving up anchor, when suddenly a monstrous cuttlefish appeared on top of the water and slung its arms about two of the masts. The tips of the arms reached to the mastheads, and the weight of the cuttle dragged the ship over, so that she lay on her beam-ends and was near to being capsized. The crew seized axes and knives, and cut away at the arms of the monster; but, despairing of escape, called upon their patron saint, Saint Thomas, to help them.
>
> Their prayers seemed to give them renewed courage, for they persevered, and finally succeeded in cutting off the arms, when the animal sank and the vessel was righted. Now, when the ship returned to St. Malo, the crew, grateful for their deliverance from so hideous a danger, marched

in procession to the chapel of their patron saint, where they offered a solemn thanksgiving, and afterwards had a painting made representing the conflict with the cuttle, and which was hung in the chapel.

Montfort had a copy made of this painting, but the artist made the whole thing seem even more fantastic. When the copy was published, the critics hooted at it and called the picture an even bigger fake than Montfort's books. He was titled "the most outrageous charlatan Paris has ever known." The original picture was taken from the chapel and no one knows whether it was hidden or destroyed.

The coast of New England was a popular place for sea monster sightings between 1815 and 1823. One of them was seen in 1815 heading south in the bay near Gloucester, Massachusetts. It was described as being about one hundred feet long. Its head looked like a horse's head, and it was dark brown.

It was said to have made another visit in 1817, and the *Gloucester Telegraph* reported: "On the 14th of August the sea serpent was approached by a boat within thirty feet, and on raising its head above water was greeted by a volley from the gun of an experienced sportsman. The creature turned directly toward the boat, as if meditating an attack, but sank down."

This sighting was the first one ever to be investigated scientifically. The Linnaean Society of New England, a group of gentlemen who were interested in natural science, decided to get more information about the Gloucester

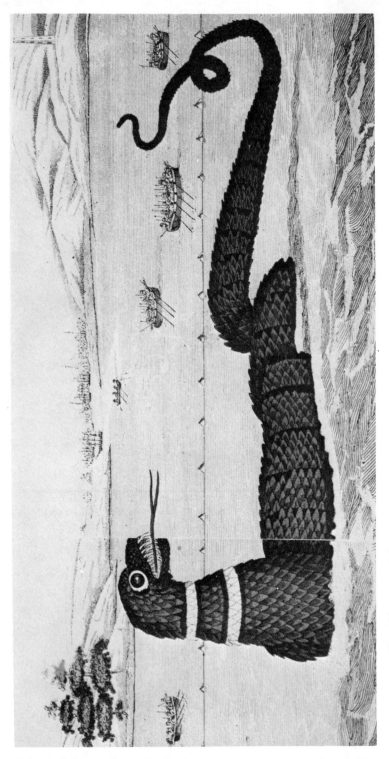

The Gloucester Monster.

Harbor Monster. They asked the local justice of the peace to take sworn depositions from the witnesses, and have them answer a questionnaire that the society had prepared. Eight of these were taken—two from ship captains, three from tradesmen, and one each from a carpenter, a sailor, and a seventeen-year-old boy.

They seemed to agree that the creature looked like a huge snake with lumps on its back. Also, it seemed to be about one hundred feet long. Sometimes it floated on the surface; sometimes it jumped around like a porpoise. Most of the time, however, it chased and ate herring.

Then the society made a mistake. They wondered what the creature was doing in water so close to shore, and decided that it wanted to lay its eggs. While the members of the society didn't find any eggs, somebody did find a dead snake, about three feet long, with a humped back. The members of the society decided that this snake was a baby sea serpent.

They dissected the snake, which they had given the scientific name *Scoliophis atlanticus*. "On the whole," they wrote, "as these two animals agree in so many conspicuous, important, and peculiar characteristics, and as no material difference between them has yet been clearly pointed out, excepting that of size, the society will probably feel justified in considering them individuals of the same species."

The baby sea serpent was really a full-grown black snake with a diseased back. Needless to say, they were criticized in the scientific journals of the day.

In 1818, the creature, or one that looked just like it, was sighted off the coast of Nahant, Massachusetts. Samuel

Cabot of Boston was standing on the beach when he observed that several boats were turning around and heading
for shore. Cabot described the scene:

> My attention was suddenly arrested by an object emerging
> from the water at the distance of about 100 or 150 yards,
> which gave to my mind at the first glance, the idea of a
> horse's head. It was elevated about two feet from the
> water, and he depressed it gradually to within six or eight
> inches as he moved along. His bunches appeared to me not
> altogether uniform in size. I felt persuaded by this exam-
> ination that he would not be less than eighty feet long.

The monster reappeared in 1819 and was seen by dozens
of people. One of them said:

> I had with me an excellent telescope, and . . . saw appear,
> at a short distance from the shore, an animal whose body
> formed a series of blackish curves, of which I counted thir-
> teen. . . . This at least I can affirm . . . that it was neither a
> whale nor a cachalot [sperm whale], nor any stronger souf-
> fleur [dolphin], nor any other enormous cetacean [water
> mammal]. None of these gigantic animals has such an un-
> dulating back.

The creature was also sighted by the captain and the
mate of the sloop *Concord*. They both made a sworn statement in front of a justice of the peace. The mate described
the monster by saying: "His head was about as long as a
horse's and was a proper snake's head—there was a degree
of flatness, with a slight hollow on the top of his head—his
eyes were prominent, and stood out considerable from the
surface. . . ."

Over the years, the Gloucester Monster was sighted many times. In 1866, for example, it was seen not only in Gloucester Harbor, but also off Cape Cod and Southport and Norwalk, Connecticut.

Olaus Magnus' maned sea serpent of 1555 seemed to make a comeback in 1848. Captain Peter M'Quhae and six members of his crew sighted the monster while they were on the deck of the H. M. S. *Daedalus*. They described the creature, and the strange part of this story is that seven experienced sailors claimed that they had observed the monster for about twenty minutes. They said that it was ". . . enormous . . . there was at least sixty feet of the animal on the surface of the water. The diameter of the serpent was about fifteen or sixteen inches behind the head, which was . . . that of a snake."

Then, about six weeks later, a similar serpent was seen by the officers and crew of the American brig, *Daphne*.

The English naturalist Henry Lee tried to explain the *Daedalus* sighting. Like Egede's Kraken, he thought that the serpent was a giant squid seen from an angle. The tail was exposed and the tentacles, as they undulated in the water, appeared to be little bumps on the surface. In his book, *Sea Monsters Unmasked*, published in 1884, Lee tried to prove that all sea serpents sighted in the past had been giant squids.

Captain William Taylor, master of the British ship *British Banner*, reported the following story in 1860:

> On the 25th of April, in lat. 12 deg. 7 min. 8 sec. N., and long. 93 deg. 52 min. E., with the sun over the mainyard, felt a strong sensation as if the ship was trembling. Sent the

second mate aloft to see what was up. The latter called out to me to go up the fore rigging and look over the bows. I did so, and saw an enormous serpent shaking the bowsprit with its mouth.

It must have been at least 300 feet long; was about the circumference of a very wide crinoline petticoat, with black back, shaggy mane, horn on the forehead, and large glaring eyes placed rather near the nose, and jaws about eight feet long. He did not observe me, and continued shaking the bowsprit and throwing the sea alongside into a foam until the former came clear away from the ship.

The serpent was powerful enough, although the ship was carrying all sail, and going at about ten knots at the time he attacked us, to stop her way completely. When the bowsprit, with the jibboom, sails, and rigging, went by the board, the monster swallowed the foretopmast, staysail, jib, and flying-jib, with the greatest apparent ease.

He shoved off a little after this, and returned apparently to scratch himself against the side of the ship, making the most extraordinary noise, resembling that on board a steamer when the boilers are blowing off. The serpent darted off like a flash of lightning, striking the vessel with its tail, and staving in all the starboard quarter gallery with its tail. Saw no more of it.

There is an arm of the sea on the west coast of Scotland called Loch Hourn. In 1872, six persons on board the cutter *Leda* saw a sea serpent there. The weather was clear, the sun was shining, and Loch Hourn was perfectly calm. The observers at times used telescopes to see the beast from distances as close as one hundred yards. It looked like a line of black humps—up to eight at a time. From time to time, it would stick its head above the surface of the water. Estimates of its length ran to sixty feet. When the thing was moving through the water, only the head could be seen, followed by a wide wake.

The *London Times* reported a sea monster story on July 4, 1874. The steamer *Strathowen*, bound for India, sighted on a calm sea about an hour after dusk a small schooner, the *Pearl*. A dark object was seen between the schooner and the steamer, lying half-submerged on the surface. As the steamer's 200 passengers watched in horror, the dark object crawled half aboard the schooner and dragged the 150-ton vessel down into the deep.

The sea monsters kept appearing. In 1877, the captain and several of the officers on the British ship *Osbourne* sighted one off the coast of Sicily. Its head was six feet wide, and it emerged above the water on a neck thirty feet long. Its shoulders were fifteen feet wide and its flippers were fifteen feet long.

Two zoologists reported sighting a sea serpent off the coast of Brazil in 1905. One of them later said: "A great head and neck rose out of the water. The neck appeared about the thickness of a slight man's body."

In 1917, the captain of a British warship, the H. M. S. *Hilary*, sighted one off Iceland. He described it as "a sea monster with a cowlike head on a neck about twenty-eight feet long."

Monsters were sighted in the Atlantic by passengers and crews of the *Dunbar Castle* in 1930 and the *Santa Clara* in 1947. According to the captain of the *Santa Clara:* "The creature's head appeared to be about two and one-half

Even Galveston, Texas has had its sea creatures. This one was sighted near the coast.

feet across, two feet thick, and five feet long. The . . . body was about three feet thick and the neck about one and one-half feet in diameter." This creature was seen only about 118 miles east of Cape Lookout, North Carolina.

Captain John Ridgway and Sergeant Chay Blyth, while rowing across the Atlantic in their boat *English Rose III* in 1966, were almost rammed by a sea serpent. Blyth was asleep when Ridgway, who was rowing, heard a swishing sound on the starboard side of the boat. He wrote:

> I looked out into the water and suddenly saw the writhing, twisting shape of a great creature. It was outlined by the phosphorescence in the sea as if a string of neon lights were hanging from it.
>
> It was an enormous size, some thirty-five or more feet long, and it came toward me quite fast. I must have watched it for some ten seconds. It headed straight at me and disappeared right beneath me. I stopped rowing. I was frozen with terror. . . . I forced myself to turn my head to look over the port side.
>
> I saw nothing, but after a brief pause, I heard a tremendous splash. I thought this might be the head of the monster crashing into the sea after coming up for a brief look at us. I did not see the surfacing—just heard it. I am not an imaginative man, and I searched for a rational explanation for this incredible occurrence in the night as I picked up the oars and started rowing again. . . . I reluctantly had to believe that there was only one thing it could have been—a sea serpent.

A sea serpent named Caddy was supposedly sighted off Vancouver Island, Canada. The most authentic-sounding

report of Caddy was made by Judge James Thomas Brown
of Saskatchewan. He, his wife, and his daughter sighted
the monster about 150 yards from shore. He reported:

> His head [was] like a snake's [and] came out of the water
> four or five feet straight up. Six or seven feet from the
> head, one of his big coils showed clearly.
>
> The coil itself was six or seven feet long, fully a foot
> thick, perfectly round and dark in color. . . . It seemed to
> look at us for a moment and then dived. It must have been
> swimming very fast, for when it came up again, it was
> about 300 yards away. . . . I got three good looks at him.
> On one occasion he came up right in front of us.
>
> There was no question about the serpent—it was quite a
> sight. I'd think the creature was thirty-five to forty feet
> long. It was like a monstrous snake. It certainly wasn't any
> of those sea animals we know, like a porpoise, sea lion, and
> so on. I've seen them and know what they look like.

Over the years, there have been almost as many explanations of what sea monsters might be as there have been
sightings of the creatures themselves. It wouldn't be right
to ignore all the stories by saying that these monsters were
the products of imaginative minds. Too many clear-eyed,
cold-blooded scientists, sea captains, and newspaper reporters have recorded sightings of strange creatures.

Interest in sea serpents seems to have waned among the
scientific community, however. From 1872-1885, *Nature*, a
prominent British scientific journal, published nineteen ar-
ticles on the beasts. Almost a century later, it no longer
deals with such creatures.

Some scientists of the nineteenth century believed in

sea serpents, among them Sir Joseph Banks, the English naturalist; Sir William J. Hooker, the botanist and director of Kew Gardens in Britain; and the naturalist Henry Lee who was mentioned earlier. It was Lee who thought that the *Daedalus* sighting and the sighting of a Kraken could have been merely partially hidden giant squids with their heads and tentacles beneath the surface of the water and only their tails visible, standing erect.

Professor Ron Westrum of Eastern Michigan University is an expert on sea serpents. He defines them as: "Any large, elongated marine creature of an apparently unknown species." He also points out that sea serpent sightings occur, on the average, at a rate of about three per year, and this number has remained constant since 1800.

A giant pink squid was captured off the coast of Peru not long ago. It had thirty-five-foot-long tentacles and its eyes were a foot in diameter. Pieces of squid taken from the stomachs of whales may have come from animals that were more than one hundred feet in length. Some oceanographers believe that there may be other giant squids deep in the oceans that might be even larger. Could they be our sea monsters?

Dr. L. D. Brongersma of The Netherlands suggested that sea serpents were really giant turtles. He wondered why these monsters were never reported to have washed up on shore. He also pointed out that the bumps on the water seen by so many observers may just be several turtles swimming along in a line. On the other hand, they could be porpoises. A line of those sea mammals seen at a distance resembles an undulating, serpentine creature.

Some scientists think that the monsters may be sharks. In recent years, sharks have been found whose heads measure from four feet between the eyes. Even bigger fish may someday be found in the lower depths of the oceans.

Others blame the sightings on snakes. For example, the African python, which at times has been known to swallow a goat, has been known to swim from island to island looking for food. There have been occasions when these snakes have attempted to board ships in search of a resting place.

Then there is the walrus theory. Ancient Norwegian seafarers said that when a sea monster was sighted, a storm would follow. Professor Waldemar H. Lehn and Irmgard Schroeder of the University of Manitoba in Winnipeg agree. The descriptions of the monsters by the Norse sailors sound like the distorted, optical illusions of walruses or killer whales surfacing, nose up, under rare atmospheric conditions.

Suppose that these sailors were standing in a Norse longship. They would be about six feet above sea level and looking at something about a mile away. If there were an atmospheric inversion (a warm air layer under a cold air layer), the conditions would be perfect for such an optical illusion. A walrus would become a pillarlike monster with long, cruel fangs. And these conditions could have occurred only in the last stages of a warm front in a calm just before a storm. The old Norsemen were right.

One of the most experienced believers in sea monsters is Dr. Anton Bruun. This Danish marine biologist, so respected that an oceanographic vessel bears his name, outlined a theory about these creatures of the deep.

In 1962, he described one of his own experiences. While

A mysterious, forty-foot-long marine animal was washed ashore in January 1950 near Suez, in Egypt. Zoologists were puzzled by the species of dead "monster," which had long, sharp tusks. (WIDE WORLD PHOTOS)

on a voyage in 1930, he hauled up some sampling nets and found a huge eel larva. He knew that the largest eels grow to about ten feet in length and weigh one hundred pounds or more. Normally, when an eel is in the larval stage, it is about five inches long. The giant eel larva that Bruun found measured about six feet in length.

Bruun estimated that if it became full-grown, it might measure fifty feet in length. Perhaps this kind of giant eel is our sea monster. The larva was found about two miles below the surface of the water, and this may be why we seldom see them. Bruun made no definite statement, but left the door open for further searches into the frigid depths of the oceans.

What do we really know about life beneath the surface of the seas? Not much. We have been exploring those areas for only a bit over one hundred years. In 1865, a Frenchman descended to a depth of 245 feet. On January 23, 1960, Dr. Jacques Piccard and Lieutenant D. Walsh of the United States Navy went down in the bathyscaph *Trieste* into the Marianas Trench on the Pacific Ocean floor. This is the world's deepest trench; from top to bottom it is higher than Mount Everest. At a depth of 35,802 feet, they described the bottom as "waste of snuff-colored ooze." But Piccard, and later Jacques Cousteau, have seen types of fish that had been previously unknown.

It had long been thought that fish could not survive at great depths, but a research vessel found one and brought it up from 26,000 feet. At that depth, the ocean is totally black, but this fish had two primitive eyes, and it probably once lived closer to the surface.

In 1938, a South African trawler picked up a coelacanth in its net. It had been thought that this fish had lived about 300 million years ago and had been extinct for more than 70 million years. And, since trawlers generally sink their nets only about sixty feet down, where had the coelacanth come from?

Scientists want to find out. The world's largest research submarine, the *Ben Franklin,* designed by Piccard, descended to a depth of 600 feet in the Gulf Stream in 1969. The United States Navy is developing a Deep Submergence Search Vehicle with underwater television, sonar sensing equipment, and electronic flashlamps and floodlights.

Information on sightings of sea monsters taken by the United States Coast Guard were relayed to the Woods Hole Oceanographic Institute. Most of them turned out to be dead giant squids floating in the water.

Dr. C. E. LaFond of the Scripps Oceanographic Institute once reported "several large, sharklike fish" swimming at a depth of 4,000 feet in the San Diego Trough. He later said: "I hesitated to tell anyone about them because they had eyes as big as dinner plates."

The point is that about 200 million years ago, the oceans were probably full of monsters—huge sharks, crabs, sea serpents, lungfish, skates, and rays. Many of them had body armor and stingers. Who are we, who know very little about the depths of the seas, to say that all of them became extinct? Could they still be living down there, coming to the surface only at irregular intervals to frighten the unwary sailor?

NESSIE

LOCH Ness is a large lake in the northern part of Scotland, running in a southwesterly direction from Inverness. It is also the largest freshwater lake, by volume, in Great Britain and the third largest in Europe. Located in the Great Glen—the major geological fault that spans Scotland—it is fifty-two feet above sea level, twenty-two and one-half miles long, and one and three-quarter miles wide at its widest point.

In the early part of the nineteenth century, it was joined with two other lochs—Oich and Lochy—to form the Caledonian Canal. For centuries it was thought to be bottomless, but this belief was disproved in the early part of the twentieth century.

It is deep, though. The average depth along the center line of the lake is about 500 feet, and there is one point where a sounding will reveal a depth of 734 feet. Because of its depth, the loch never freezes to any great extent. Its temperature hovers around 42° F. all year and rarely goes below 35° F.

The bottom is covered with either thick mud or stiff, yellow clay, except for two places that are bare rock. The water is so murky with suspended peat particles that the maximum underwater visibility is only a few feet. In many places, when one puts a hand into the water, the fingers cannot be seen. The water at the bottom is anaerobic, which means that there is no oxygen to support life as we know it. This condition also has the effect that when an object falls to the bottom—including people who have drowned—it never returns to the surface.

In the primitive past, the residents around the loch would sacrifice animals to a creature that was supposed to be living in Loch Ness. Of course, these animals were never seen again. So the stories about the Loch Ness Monster increased as the years went by.

Perhaps the tale really begins in the year 565, when the Irish missionary Saint Columba was walking along the edge of the loch. He had been trying to convert the heathen Picts, Scots, and Northumbrians from his monastery on the Island of Iona off the western coast of Scotland. But on a trip through the northern part of the country, he came upon Loch Ness.

When Saint Columba arrived at the loch, he found some of the local people burying a townsman who had been mauled by the lake monster and later died of his wounds. One of the followers of the missionary, a man named Lugne, swam across the narrows at the head of the loch to bring back a small boat that had been left on the other side.

As he was swimming, he suddenly came face to face with "a very odd-looking beastie, something like a huge frog, only it was not a frog." The monster swam toward the man and would have attacked him if Saint Columba had not intervened. The missionary shouted at the monster: "Go thou no further nor touch the man. Go back at once!"

According to a biography of the saint written in the eighth century: "On hearing this word . . . the monster was terrified and fled away again more quickly than if it had been dragged on by ropes, though it approached Lugne as he swam so closely that between man and monster there was no more than the length of one punt pole." You can believe that the natives were astonished at Saint Columba's power, and many of them converted to Christianity on the spot.

The legend says that Saint Columba did such good work that the Loch Ness Monster was not seen again until the late 1800s. Even so, at the beginning of the 1800s, the monster was so feared that children were warned not to play on the banks of the loch.

Of all people, that level-headed Scottish author Sir Walter Scott wrote of the monster. In November of 1827, he declared:

> Clanronald told us . . . that a set of his kinsmen—believing that the fabulous "water-cow" inhabited a small lake near his house—resolved to drag the monster into day. With this in view, they bivouacked by the side of the lake in which

they placed, by way of nightbait, two small anchors such as belong to boats, each baited with the carcass of a dog, slain for the purpose. They expected the water-cow would gorge on the bait and were prepared to drag her to shore the next morning when, to their confusion, the baits were found untouched.

In 1880, a diver named Duncan McDonald was trying to salvage a boat wrecked on the loch when he came across the creature. "I was underwater about my work," he said, "when all of a sudden the monster swam by me as cool and calm as you please. She paid no heed to me, but I got a glance at one of her eyes as she went by. It was small, gray, and baleful. I would not have liked to displease or anger her in any way."

Since that time, the Loch Ness Monster, nicknamed "Nessie," has been sighted by more than 4,000 people. Ninety percent of these sightings occurred when the lake was calm. For some reason, the animal has always been thought of as being female. She was also given a scientific name by a scientist, Sir Peter Scott. He called her *Nessiteras rhombopteryx*, which means "Ness marvel with diamond-shaped fin."

Most of these sightings describe her as a dark-gray or brownish-black creature with a long, slender neck, a small head, a heavy body, a long powerful tail, and four diamond-shaped paddles or fins. The number of humps may vary from one to three. She is fifteen to twenty feet long, and her head has angular protuberances.

Following McDonald's sighting, there were a few others, most notably in 1912, 1927, and 1930. But it was in 1933

that Nessie became an international pet. That was also the
year that a new road was built on the northern shore of the
loch between Fort William and Inverness.

Local people think that Nessie was awakened by the
drilling of the road crew, the noise of the explosions, and
the huge stones that fell into the lake. An automobile
association policeman spotted her and described her as "a
thing with a number of humps above the water line. . . . It
had a small head and a very long, slender neck."

The year of 1933 was a big one for sightings. On May 2,
a correspondent for the Inverness *Courier*, wrote of the
experience of Mr. and Mrs. John Makay. They said that
they had seen "an enormous animal rolling and plunging"
in Loch Ness. It is said that the editor of the *Courier* was
the one who christened the beast the "Loch Ness Monster."

On July 22, a London businessman and his wife, Mr.
and Mrs. George Spicer, were driving back to London
from their vacation in the Scottish Highlands. At 4 P.M.,
they were at a point halfway between Doyes and Foyer on
the south bank of Loch Ness. Mrs. Spicer noticed something moving out from the bushes on the hillside.

As they watched, a creature with a long neck and a huge
body, dark gray like an elephant, lumbered across the road.
Mr. Spicer said that it looked like a huge snail with a long
neck and must have measured from twenty-five to thirty
feet long. Also, it was carrying what looked like a lamb in
its mouth. It plunged down the bank and disappeared into
the water.

On November 13, Hugh Gray, an employee of the British Aluminium Company, took what was probably the first

picture of what was claimed to be the monster from about 200 feet away. He had taken five shots of the beast, but four of the negatives turned out to be blank. The fifth was cloudy, but an official of the Kodak Company attested that it had not been tampered with in any way. It was published in the Scottish *Daily Record* and reproduced all over the world.

But most scientists were unconvinced. J. R. Norman of the British Museum stated that "the possibilities leveled down to the object being a bottle-nosed whale, one of the larger species of shark, or just mere wreckage." Professor Graham Kerr of the University of Glasgow described the photo as being "unconvincing as a representation of a living creature."

Also in November, the British House of Commons got into the act. A member of Parliament demanded an official investigation to settle "the monster matter."

Journalists from all parts of the world gathered at the loch. There were writers and photographers from New York, Rio de Janeiro, and Tokyo, to name a few. Boy Scouts were enlisted to help watch for the monster. All in all, there were fifty-two reported sightings in 1933 alone.

After the Spicers' sighting, the loch became a favorite vacation spot for tourists. Many people claimed that they had seen Nessie and heard her make sounds of anger or anguish. But these stories made no impression on E. G. Boulenger, the director of the aquarium at the London Zoo. He wrote:

> The case of the Loch Ness Monster is worthy of our consideration if only because it presents a striking example of

mass hallucination. . . . For countless centuries a wealth of weird and eerie legend has centered around this great inland waterway. . . . Any person with the slightest knowledge of human nature should therefore find no difficulty in understanding how an animal, once said to have been seen by a few persons, should shortly after have revealed itself to many more.

Other reasons for all these sightings were offered by some disbelievers. They pointed out that there were rewards being offered for the live capture of Nessie. A New York zoo was giving $500, Bertram Mills Circus in England had offered £20,000, and the makers of Black and White whiskey in Scotland had offered the huge sum of £1 million.

The excitement continued into 1934. On April 21, the London *Daily Mail* published a photograph of the monster taken by a London physician, Dr. Robert Kenneth Wilson. He was driving home from a vacation in northern Scotland and stopped his car at 7:30 A.M. to stretch his legs by the lake.

Wilson was parked on one of the slopes around the lake about 200 feet above its surface. The water began to swirl and he saw "the head of some strange animal rising." He ran to his car to get his camera, which had a telephoto lens, returned, and took four pictures. Two of them were no good, but the third showed the monster's long neck and the fourth showed its small head about to submerge. No evidence of faking the pictures could be found.

One odd event took place that year. Malcolm Irvine of Scottish Film Productions had taken what he claimed was the first movie of Nessie on December 12, 1933. This was shown to a private audience in London in 1934. For some strange reason, this film disappeared before it could be checked for authenticity.

In the summer of 1934, the first book about Nessie was published. It was *The Loch Ness Monster and Others,* written by Rupert Gould, a retired naval officer who had spent time at the loch during the previous year. Actually, it was a collection of forty-seven sighting records, complete with drawings and photographs.

Between July and August, the first serious investigative expedition was conducted at Loch Ness. It operated under the sponsorship of Sir Edward Mountain, an insurance millionaire. Several sightings were made, and a film was taken by Captain James Frazier of Inverness. However, zoologists who saw the movie agreed that the creature was probably a seal.

Then came World War II, and Nessie dropped out of the news until the 1950s. In the late 1950s, the British Broadcasting Company sent a television team to the loch. The BBC's team was equipped with a sonic depth-finder, and a mysterious object was recorded some twelve feet beneath the surface and followed to a depth of sixty feet. But most scientists scoffed at this evidence.

Because of the peat silt coming from the forty-five mountain streams and five rivers that empty into the loch, very little can be seen in the water below six feet beneath the surface. So usually, when Nessie is sighted, she looks like a mere series of humps above the surface.

A film taken of Nessie in 1960 revealed these humps.

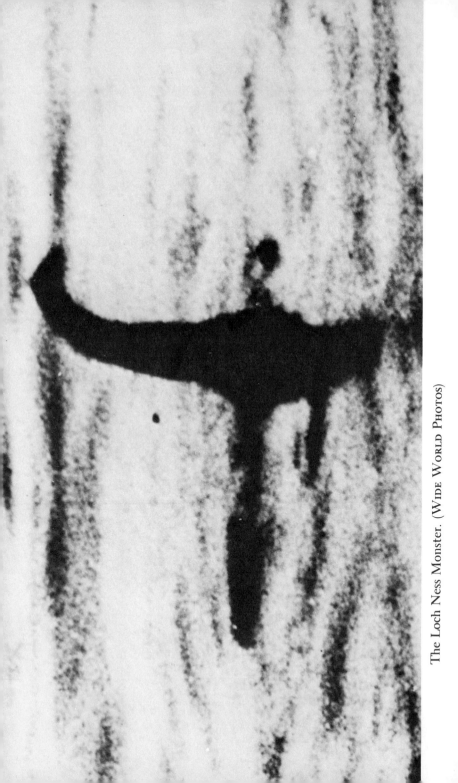

The Loch Ness Monster. (WIDE WORLD PHOTOS)

This motion picture was turned over to the Ministry of Defence's Joint Air Reconnaissance Intelligence Centre in London. The Royal Air Force had special equipment that could examine aerial reconnaissance photos and decide what was in a murky or indistinct picture.

As it turned out, they said that the film showed that something alive, "an animate object," was moving through the water—not a shadow, not a log, not a boat. And there was no evidence that could be found to indicate that the movie was a fake.

In August 1968, a team from the department of electronic engineering of the University of Birmingham, England set up a sonar system on a pier at Loch Ness. They directed the scan toward the southeast corner of the loch and came up with a sighting. The cathode display screen was photographed every ten seconds by a movie camera. At 4:30 P.M. on August 18, they had a remarkable thirteen-minute sequence.

According to an observer:

> A large object rose rapidly from the floor of the loch at a range of a half mile, its speed of ascent being about one hundred feet a minute. It was rising obliquely away from the sonar source at a velocity of about six and one-half knots [seven and one-half miles per hour], and was soon more than a half mile away. Its upward movement had now slowed to about one and one-half miles per hour. This object then changed directions to move toward the pier at about ten miles per hour, keeping constant depth. Finally, it plunged to the bottom at about one hundred feet a minute before rising again at a three and one-half mile

range, when it apparently moved out of the sonar beam and was lost to record. Meanwhile, a second large object had been detected at three-tenths of a mile from the pier which finally dived at the astonishing velocity of five miles per hour. Both objects remained many feet below the surface.

In 1969, an American encyclopedia company sponsored Dan Taylor, an American captain, and a British crew on a homemade mini-submarine expedition below the surface of the loch. Also in that year, an English newspaper sponsored a mini-submarine search. The *Pisces* could stay under the surface for twelve hours and had a sonar system. Nessie didn't show up for either of these submarines to detect her.

An expedition in 1970 used infrared cameras that permitted the scientists to take pictures in the dark at a distance of one hundred yards. A Japanese team went to Loch Ness in 1973. Still no luck.

Experts now estimate that there is about one sighting for every 350 hours spent watching Loch Ness. Who are these watchers and what are their theories?

The Loch Ness Monster has so captured the imaginations of countless people that in 1969 the Bureau for Investigating the Loch Ness Monster Phenomenon Ltd. was incorporated. Their plan was that between March 15 and October 15 every year, a large number of investigators would descend on the loch to look for Nessie. The grand total of investigators might be as high as 500 per year, plus one winter observer who was to go out every morning with a pair of binoculars to pursue his cold, lonely vigil.

The bureau was to run a strictly scientific operation. When the summer visitors arrived, they would scan the surface of the lake with thirty-five millimeter cameras equipped with telephoto lenses. They would hunt in boats powered by silent electric motors and equipped with floodlights and crossbow harpoons. They added sonar in 1968—a new kind of sonar whose echoes were fed through a computer.

There were numerous problems connected with the search. The most difficult was money. The volunteers, each of whom spent two weeks at the loch each year, were not paid. As a matter of fact, they had to pay for their own transportation and camp out while they were there. What little money there was came from membership dues and various business and industrial sources.

Another problem was the size of the loch. It is too big. The bureau could patrol and survey only about three-quarters of its surface every summer.

In 1966, Dr. Roy Mackal, a professor of biochemistry at the University of Chicago, was appointed director of the Loch Ness Investigation Bureau. Dr. Mackal is a scientist with a Ph.D. in biochemistry from the University of Chicago. Before he became interested in Nessie, he had been doing research on DNA.

As a true scientist would do when confronted with additional information, Mackal was willing to change his hypotheses from time to time. For example, he suggested in 1966 that the monster was a sort of sea slug.

In 1969, he said that Nessie might be an overgrown, freshwater-adapted sea cow. His reasoning followed a scientific explanation for finding sea monsters in an inland body of water. After the Ice Age retreated—5,000 to 7,000 years ago—many lakes were cut off from the sea. Gradually, the water turned fresh. And, according to one theory, a large aquatic animal could have been trapped in the newly formed lakes and forced to adapt to the conditions or die.

Mackal said that gigantic worms or even squid would not have the bone structure to match the principal description of Nessie—thirty-five feet long, slender neck, flippers, tapering tail, and small head and eyes.

So the sea cow offered the best explanation. Warm-water sea cows, such as the dugong of Australia and the manatee of Florida rivers and the Caribbean, follow behavior patterns similar to Nessie. And a species of sea cow thirty-five-feet long was discovered in the eighteenth century. They have long been thought to be extinct, but who knows?

In 1976, Mackal also said that Nessie might be a plesiosaur, an animal that dates back 100 million years. This dinosaur had a barrel-shaped body and a snakelike neck. No one knows when or if the sea dinosaurs became extinct. Could they be living in the deepest parts of the sea or in Loch Ness?

Is it possible that a plesiosaur could still be alive? In 1977, Japanese fishermen off the coast of New Zealand netted a dead animal that they could not identify. They hauled up part of the creature—the part weighed two tons and was forty-four-feet long—and took a few samples and photographs. But the thing smelled so bad that the fishermen returned the rotting creature to the sea.

Professor Yoshinori Imiazumi, the director of animal research at the Japanese National Science Museum, examined the photos and a drawing of the dead animal and said that it looked like a plesiosaurus and almost certainly was a reptile. Tokio Shikama, who has been described as a scholar of ancient animals at Yokohama National University, said: "It has to be a plesiosaurus."

Professor Fujio Yasuda of the Tokyo Fisheries University also said that the photos looked like a plesiosaurus, but he could not be sure without a bone sample.

On the other hand, A. Fraser-Brunner, a Scottish zoologist and aquarium curator of the Royal Zoological Society of Scotland, was positive that the carcass was that of a Hooker's sea lion. Carl Stubbs of the Scripps Institute of Oceanography thought that it was probably a small whale, and his colleague, Richard Rosenblatt, added that "dead whales have been identified as all sorts of things."

Stubbs doubted that any unknown ancient reptile could exist in the ocean because it would need to surface frequently for air and so would not really be unknown. He declared: "If I'm wrong, I'd like to know."

Fraser-Brunner added: "They [plesiosaurs] could not exist in cold, deep waters. Moreover, plesiosaurs laid eggs as turtles do, and if that was happening in Loch Ness, the Scots already would be marketing the eggs."

Another British scientist, Dr. Maurice Burton, disagreed with the plesiosaur theory. He felt that Nessie might be a mammal, but not a sea cow. Burton projected Gray's 1933 photograph on a screen and concluded that the beast was actually an otter on the surface of the water. He also looked at some pictures taken in 1963 and felt that they were taken of the tail of an otter who was playfully diving into the water.

On the other hand, Dr. George R. Zug, curator of reptiles and amphibians at the Smithsonian Institution, thinks Nessie might be a fish rather than a mammal or a reptile. He points out that she is rarely seen on the surface. An air-breathing monster would have to surface regularly to breathe.

Another organization that has searched for Nessie is the Boston Academy of Applied Science Team, headed by Dr. Robert H. Rines. Rines first took photos in the murky waters of Loch Ness in 1972. He submerged a camera and strobe system forty-five feet below the surface of the water and triggered it when sonar indicated that the monster was in camera view. The resulting photos were computer-enhanced, but were still puzzling.

In 1975, the team was back at the loch for another study that was partially financed by *The New York Times*. They used an underwater stroboscopic camera and obtained sonar and photographic images of a large, solid animal with flippers. The engineer who performed the computer enhancement of these photographs, Alan Gillespie of the California Institute of Technology's Jet Propulsion Laboratory, said:

> One picture showed a body with a long neck and two stubby appendages. . . . The second frame appeared to show a neck and head, with the head closer to the camera than the body . . . the neck was reticulated.
>
> The head supported projections. . . . I see no evidence that they are a picture of a model, toy, or whatever. I

emphasize: I detect no evidence of a fraud. These objects are not patterns of algae, sediment, or gas bubbles.

The photos taken in Loch Ness were published in 1975 by the respected British journal *Nature,* and more data were to be found in *Technology Review,* published by the Massachusetts Institute of Technology, and *The MCZ Newsletter,* published by Harvard University's Museum of Comparative Zoology. Professors at Harvard, MIT, and scientists from the Smithsonian Institution, the Royal Ontario Museum at Toronto, Canada, the New England Aquarium, and the National History Museum of London were intrigued.

A panel set up by the British Museum of Natural History was not convinced, however. The panel ruled: "None of the photographs is sufficiently informative to establish the existence, far less the identity, of a large living animal in the loch."

Gillespie argued with that. "There is unquestionably a real object in the loch's murky waters." But he didn't identify it as an unknown creature, a known animal species, or a hoax.

Then the team made a statement:

> Although we make no claim to being expert zoologists, we can find no combination of phenomena that account for these data as well as the simple explanation that a large creature inhabits the loch. Not even the experts have offered a plausible alternative explanation, in our view. In addition, there have been other investigations which suggest that the loch is capable of supporting a breeding population of such animals, and that physiological adaptation

to the cold loch waters is feasible for a wide variety of candidate species.

Roy Mackal certainly agreed with part of that statement. According to him, there are enough salmon in Loch Ness to support at least two dozen monsters.

Rines suffered a couple of setbacks in 1979. He had planned to equip two dolphins with cameras and strobelights in order to have them seek out the monster. But this did not happen because of the death of one of the dolphins. Then, in August, two women saw a creature with a serpentlike head and enormous body swimming just off Urquhart Bay's Temple Pier, the area of Loch Ness where Rines usually had his underwater cameras. The cameras, however, had been found to be defective and had been sent back to the United States for repair.

By 1977, Mackal had developed three hypotheses about Nessie. He thought that perhaps she was an amphibian because sightings had occurred in Loch Ness, Loch Oich, Loch Lochy, and Loch Linnhe. None had been reported from Moray Firth. Moray Firth is quite salty, and almost all amphibians are unable to live in salt water.

Eels were another possibility, as were ancient reptiles. He discounted mammals because they would have to come to the surface to breathe, and the lake monsters are not sighted that often.

Mackal hoped to capture the monster and isolate it for a time so that it could be studied. He said:

> We know it will be perfectly happy out of the water for a few minutes, at least, where we can make clear photographs, scrape a little skin for immunological investigation,

measure the anatomical features, and of course positively identify the animal. And then we should return it to the lake.

But I ought to be fair. This is a fishing expedition. At this point there isn't much science involved. It's a matter of whether or not we can get the animals to take our bait and animals are notorious about not doing things to suit our convenience. All in all, I'm pretty optimistic. I think we're on the verge of hitting some real scientific pay dirt.

One of the strangest theories is that Nessie is really a swimming elephant. Dennis Johnson of the University of Illinois was studying how elephants swim. His object was to explain how the woolly mammoth crossed from America to the northern Channel Islands off the coast of southern California during the Pleistocene times.

Scientists think a complete land bridge at that time did not exist, so the animals must have been able to swim across. After all, there have been reports of long-distance swims by elephants off the coasts of India, Bangladesh, and Kenya, so why not long-distance swims by their ancestors?

One of Johnson's associates, Dennis Power of the Santa Barbara, California Museum of Natural History, noticed that a photo of an elephant swimming, taken by R. Kadirgamar in the waters off Sri Lanka, looked like the Nessie photo taken by Wilson in 1934. The trunk and partially submerged head resembled a long neck and humped body. There is no way of guessing how an elephant got into Loch Ness. Perhaps it had escaped from a circus.

Regardless of all the controversy, we might well consider

a statement made by Dr. Robert H. Rines, who was the leader of the Academy of Applied Science Team that investigated Loch Ness in 1972. He told a radio reporter: "We wouldn't have been here if we didn't have the suspicion that there is something very large in this loch. My own view now, after having personal interviews with, I think, highly reliable people, is that there is an amazing scientific discovery awaiting the world here in Loch Ness."

6 OTHER CREATURES IN THE WATER

THE water monster with the longest pedigree in the United States is probably the monster of Lake Champlain, who is called "Champ" by the chamber of commerce in Port Henry, New York. Lake Champlain forms part of the border between New York State and Vermont. It is 100 miles long and reaches depths of 700 feet. And like Loch Ness, it was once an arm of the sea.

In 1609, Samuel de Champlain, the French discoverer of the lake, wrote of seeing a swimming monster. He told of a creature twenty feet long, as thick as a barrel, with a horse-shaped head: "A great long monster, lying in the lake, allowing birds to land on its back, then snapping them in whole." Since that time, the creature has been seen more than a hundred times—five times in 1980 alone.

Perhaps more sightings have occurred than that. Mrs. Robert A. Green claimed that she had seen a "super-long thing with three humps" in the lake, but when she told her friends about it all they did was laugh. She also implied that many other people had seen the thing but were afraid to admit it for fear of ridicule.

One person who wasn't afraid was Walter F. Wojewodzic, a retired mine worker. In 1980, he said:

> Dick Gilbo from over at Gilbo's Hardware and I were coming in from duck hunting five or six years ago when we spotted about 300 yards out in Bulwagga Bay three gray humps about three feet high moving along making quite a wake. The whole thing was about forty feet long and we couldn't even see a head. We watched it for about a minute and a half as it traveled a few hundred feet. Then it dived.
>
> The lake was as smooth as glass that day. I've fished this lake for forty-five years and I can tell you it wasn't any kind of wave, fish, or animal I ever saw. There's something big in that lake—awful big.

Bess Sherlock lives on the shore of the lake. She saw the monster, too, and said: "I saw it right out there. Like everybody else, I kept my mouth shut because I thought people would think I was crazy. In a year or two, I guess I could get ten or fifteen dollars for that view from the tourists. Maybe I could rent binoculars."

A photo of the creature was taken in 1977 by Mrs. Sandra Mansi of New Haven, Connecticut. The photograph was taken while she and her husband Anthony and their children were on a picnic on the shore of the lake. Mansi said he had gone to the car to get the camera and returned to the shore to find his children wading happily in the water and his wife in a panic. The creature had surfaced about 150 feet from shore. He related: "I threw her the camera and said, 'Take a picture and let's get out of here.' "

The picture showed a tiny image of a creature with a long neck, a humped back, and a flipper. It was run through the computer-imaging equipment at Kitt Peak National Observatory near Tucson, Arizona. The results showed that the picture had not been faked, and that the object was surfacing rather than just bobbing or floating along in the lake.

A few explanations were offered. Some scientists said that the monster was really an unusual wave or a sturgeon, which can grow very large. Others blamed otters. Dr. Roy Mackal said that it might be a zeuglodon—a long, serpentine, whalelike creature thought to have been extinct for 20 million years. He also said that our old friend Nessie might be such a beast.

At any rate, in 1980, officials of Port Henry declared the waters of Lake Champlain off-limits to anyone who would try to harm or even tease the Lake Champlain Monster.

On August 29, 1981, both scientists and monster lovers convened in Shelburne, Vermont to debate the existence of the Lake Champlain Monster. The conference was sponsored by an organization called the Lake Champlain Committee, and was billed as a seminar on the subject, "Does Champ Exist?"

Roy Mackal held out for his theory of an ancient mammal. Richard Greenwell of the University of Arizona, who had analyzed the Mansi photo, said that if such a creature existed, it was probably a plesiosaurus. Dr. George Zug, chairman of the department of vertebrate zoology at the Smithsonian Institution National Museum of Natural History, noted that evidence was mounting that some creature inhabited the cold lakes of the Northern Hemisphere.

In 1765, the *Gentleman's Magazine* of London printed a story that read: "The people of Stockholm report that a great dragon, named Necker, infests the neighboring lake, and seizes and devours such boys as go into the water to wash." The lake was Lake Mälaren. The article also told that the bishop of Avranches decided to test this story by going for a swim in the lake one sunny day. The onlookers, it was said, "were greatly surprised when they saw him return from imminent danger."

There seems to have been another lake monster in Sweden in Lake Storsjön near Östersund. On the island of Forso, there is an ancient stone in the lake with a sketch of a beast with a long neck and flippers. It seems the creature was most active from 1820 to 1898, and an expedition tried to capture it with traps in 1894.

Lake Storsjö in Sweden is also a haunt of a monster. It is said that it has a white mane and is reddish in color, looking like a large sea horse. It was first seen by some farmers in 1839 and has been sighted several times over the years. The swimming speed of the creature was estimated to be at least forty-five miles per hour.

In 1946, three people claimed to have seen the monster, saying that the lake's surface "was broken by a giant, snakelike object with three prickly, dark humps. It swam at a good parallel to the shore, on which the waves caused by the object were breaking." There were more sightings in 1965.

In the middle of the nineteenth century, lakes in Canada seemed to furnish a number of sightings of monsters. One of the most famous was Ogopogo or, as he was known to the Indians, Naitaka.

While taking a team of horses on a raft across Lake Okanagan in British Columbia in 1854, an Indian came in contact with this monster. He claimed to have been "seized by a giant hand which tried to pull me down into the water." He got away, but the horses weren't as lucky. The multi-armed creature pulled all of them under the water and drowned them.

Ogopogo seemed to be particularly fond of horses. A pioneer named John McDougal said that he had gone through the same type of experience as had the Indian. He lived, but his horses were drowned.

Early in the twentieth century, a captain in the Canadian Fishery Patrol saw the monster and described it as being like "a telegraph pole with a sheep's head." An American was said to have been struck dumb with horror on seeing it.

Ogopogo was supposedly sighted on July 2, 1919 by the Watson family of Montreal and their friend Mr. Kray. The story appeared in the newspapers: "What the party saw was a long sinuous body, thirty feet in length, consisting of about five undulations, apparently separated from

each other by about a two-foot space. . . . The length of
each of the undulations . . . would have been about five
feet. There appeared to be a forked tail, of which only
one-half came above the water."

By the 1920s, Ogopogo was so famous that a song was
composed in London:

> His mother was an earwig
> His father was a whale
> A little bit of head
> And hardly any tail
> And Ogopogo was his name.

Ogopogo was supposedly sighted by R. H. Millar, the
owner-publisher of the Vernon *Advertiser*. He wrote this
description for his paper's issue of July 20, 1959:

> Returning from a cruise down Okanagan Lake, traveling at
> ten miles an hour, I noticed, about 250 feet in our wake,
> what appeared to be the serpent. On picking up the field
> glasses, my thought was verified. It was Ogopogo, and it
> was traveling a great deal faster than we were. I would
> judge around fifteen to seventeen miles an hour.
>
> The head was about nine inches above the water. The
> head is definitely snakelike with a blunt nose. . . . Our
> excitement was short-lived. We watched for about three
> minutes, as Ogie did not appear to like the boat coming on
> him broadside; [he] very gracefully reduced the five humps
> which were so plainly visible, lowered his head, and gradu-
> ally submerged. At no time was the tail visible. The fam-
> ily's version of the color is very dark greenish. . . . This sea

serpent glides gracefully in a smooth motion. . . . This would lead one to believe that in between the humps it possibly has some type of fin which it works . . . to control direction.

Ogopogo was again sighted in February 1977. Bruce and George Elliott (aged fourteen and sixteen years) of Kelowna, British Columbia and John McNation and John McNaughton (both sixteen years old) of Rutland, British Columbia claimed to have seen the surfacing of two or three black, humplike protrusions and a sizeable wake.

Ogopogo apparently has many Canadian brothers and sisters. There is Manipogo, a serpent with a bellow like a train whistle, in Lake Winnipeg. There are Igopogo, the dog-faced monster in Lake Simcoe, forty miles north of Toronto, and T-Zum-A in Lake Shuswap, British Columbia. And don't forget Hapyxelor in Muskrat Lake, sixty miles northwest of Ottawa.

The first appearance of the Great Sea Serpent of Silver Lake occurred in 1855. A party of six, four men and two boys, were fishing on that lake in northwestern New York State. They thought that they saw a large log off the stern of their boat, but it turned out to be the head of "a most horrid and repulsive-looking monster." It seemed to be thrashing about, and its waves nearly swamped the boat.

Monster hunters seemed to be attracted by the story. Two days later, Charles Hall and his family were out on the lake when the creature rose up alongside their boat. They all "sat quietly in the boat and looked at it. It appeared to be of a dark color at first, but as it moved off going into the water, it was of a lighter color, of a copper color. . . . Its head and forward part was above the water at least a yard and upon its back it appeared to have a fin as wide as father's hand. . . . Its head was as much as fifteen or sixteen inches around and its back was much larger. . . . It [the head] was as large as a calf's head."

Nobody suspected that it might be a hoax at that time, however. But a man named A. B. Walker owned a hotel in Perry, New York that was the only one anywhere near Silver Lake. Business had not been good, but after the sightings of the monster, it was booming. Everyone wanted to stay over in hope of seeing the creature.

Then, in 1857, Walker's hotel burned down. The Perry firemen found in the ruins something that looked suspiciously like the remains of a large model of a sea serpent. Walker left town.

The model of the monster was about sixty feet long and was made from waterproof canvas. The canvas was supported by a coiled wire frame. A rubber hose was attached to the serpent that ran under the water to a shack on the shore, where it was hooked up to a bellows. All Walker had to do was sink the model in the lake, and when he wanted it to rise, he would activate the bellows. Air would go into the body and the serpent would rise. The motions of the model were directed with ropes from the serpent to the shore.

Lake serpents have been sighted in Utah, too. In 1860, *The Deseret News* of Salt Lake City told of the monster of Bear Lake. The Shoshone Indians had seen this "beast of the storm spirits" for years, but they were not taken seriously. The newspaper this time, however, wrote of a respected local citizen who had been on a horseback ride on the eastern shore of the lake. It was reported:

> About half-way, he saw something in the lake which . . . he thought to be a drowned person. . . . He rode the beach and the waves were running pretty high. . . . In a few minutes . . . some kind of an animal that he had never seen before . . . raised out of the water. He did not see the body, only the head and what he supposed to be part of the neck. It had ears or bunches on the side of its head nearly as big as a pint cup. The waves at times would dash over its head, when it would throw water from its mouth or nose. It did not drift landward, but was apparently stationary, with the exception of turning its head.

On July 28, the next day, the monster was seen by four other people. But this time it was moving and swam "much faster than a horse could run on land." Reports of the Bear Lake Monster continued for several decades.

Also in 1860, the English clergyman and author Sabine Baring-Gould wrote of the Skrimsl of Iceland. It was supposed to be fifty feet long and might have been a relative of Nessie. Baring-Gould wrote: "I should have been inclined to set the whole story down as a myth, were it not for the fact that the accounts of all the witnesses tallied with remarkable minuteness, and the monster is said to have been seen not in one portion of the lake [the Lagarflot] only, but at different points."

Baring-Gould also told of the slimy, gray-brown animal that had been seen in Lake Suldal in Norway. The head was described as being as big as a rowboat. There was a story about a man who was crossing the lake in a small boat when his arm was grasped by the mouth of the monster. He was released only after he had recited the Lord's Prayer, but his arm was so mangled that it was useless to him from then on.

Dr. Farquhar Matheson and his wife were sailing one

Sailors, it seems, have always been believers in monsters. Can you blame this one for saying a little prayer? The engraving was made more than one hundred years ago.

day in 1893 on Loch Alsh in Scotland. The weather was beautiful and the time was a little after two in the afternoon. Dr. Matheson later wrote:

> I saw something rise out of the loch in front of us—a long, straight necklike thing as tall as my mast . . . it was then 200 yards away, and it was moving toward us.
>
> Then it began to draw its neck down, and I saw clearly that it was a large sea monster. . . . It was brown in color, shining and with a sort of ruffle at the junction of its head and neck. . . . It moved its head from side to side, and I saw the reflection of the light from its wet skin.
>
> When it appeared a second time, it was going from us, and traveling at a great rate. . . . I was interested, and followed it. From its first to its last appearance we traveled a mile, and the last time we saw the thing it was about a mile away.
>
> I saw no body—only the ripple of water where the line of the body should be. I should judge, however, that there must have been a large base of body to support such a neck. It was . . . of the nature of a gigantic lizard, I should think. An eel could not lift up its body like that.

These are hardly the words of an hysterical observer.

Twenty miles from Loch Ness is Loch Morar. It, too, has its monster. Named Morag, this creature was first sighted in 1895. The dweller in the deepest lake in Britain also has had a song written about it:

> *Morag, harbinger of the deep*
> *Giant swimmer in deep-green Morar*
> *The loch which has no bottom*
> *There it is Morag the monster lives.*

In 1969, it was supposedly sighted by two fishermen. An aquatic biologist, Elizabeth Campbell, described the incident: "The two fishermen were on the loch, when they saw a black-brown hump moving toward their boat through the water. The hump was about eighteen inches above water level and a huge dark shape could be seen below. The monster rammed the boat. One of the fishermen attempted to beat it off with an oar, but the oar snapped in half when it struck the monster."

Duncan McDonnell, one of the fishermen, said, "Its skin was like that of an eel, only rougher in texture. I do not believe it came to attack us and I do not believe it is a monster. I think it is some sort of an overgrown eel."

In 1970, Dr. Neill Bass, a British biologist, headed a team to survey the loch. On the afternoon of July 14, Bass and two members of the team were taking a walk on the north shore. The surface of the loch was broken by a "black, smooth-looking, hump-shaped object," according to the scientist. A second disturbance was followed by "a spreading circular wake or ripple which radiated across the waves to about fifty yards' diameter."

In August, Alan Butterworth, a zoology student, said he sighted the monster through his binoculars. He claimed to have seen a "dark-colored hump." It was, he said, "shaped like a dome and looked like a rocky inlet."

In 1913, the German government sent a special expedition to the Cameroons in Africa. Led by Captain Freiherr von Stein, the object of the expedition was to map the territory. Von Stein wrote that the people who lived by the rivers told him of a mysterious beast that lived in the waters. It was of a "brownish-gray color with a smooth skin, its size approximately that of an elephant. . . . It is said to have a long and very flexible neck and only one tooth, but a very long one: some say it is a horn. A few spoke about a long muscular tail like that of an alligator."

Ivan T. Sanderson has been described as a first-rate naturalist whose works are respected all over the world. In 1932, he was in a canoe on the Mainyu River in West Africa. In a canoe in front of him was his fellow explorer, Gerald Russell. Accompanying them were two African aides, Ben and Bassi.

Then, as Sanderson wrote, something astonishing happened:

> The most terrible noise I have ever heard short of an oncoming earthquake or the explosion of an aerial torpedo at close range, suddenly burst forth from one of the big caves on my right. Something enormous rose out of the water. . . . This "thing" was shiny black and was the *head* of something, shaped like a seal but flattened from above to below.

Natives later told him that what he had seen was the M'koo. Sanderson also said that if those creatures lived in that river all the time, it explained why there were no crocodiles or hippos in the Mainyu River, while there were hundreds of both in the nearby rivers.

The first sighting of the White River Monster occurred in the vicinity of Newport, Arkansas in 1937. Bramlett Bateman, a plantation owner, swore that he had seen the thing several times:

I saw something appear on the surface about 375 feet away. From the best I could tell, from the distance, it was about twelve feet long and five feet wide. I did not see either head or tail but it slowly rose to the surface and stayed in this position for some five minutes. It did not move up or down the river at this time, but afterward on different occasions I have seen it move up and down the river.

Several thousand people descended on Newport that year to catch a glimpse of the monster. Some of them even paid twenty-five cents each to stand in a fenced area near the river and look. But the monster never appeared.

Then the Newport Chamber of Commerce hired a diver from Memphis to descend to the bottom of the river to see what he could find. He was down for seventy-five minutes, but saw nothing.

Over the years, the White River Monster was reportedly seen by several people. According to an unnamed witness:

I just saw a creature the size of a boxcar thrashing in the White River. . . . It was smooth, gray, and long . . . very, very long. It didn't really have scales, but from where I was standing on the shore, about 150 feet away, it looked as if the thing was peeling all over. But it was a smooth type of skin or flesh. . . . The thing was about the length of three or four pickup trucks, and at least two yards across. . . . Water began to boil up about two or three feet high, then this huge form rolled up and over; it just kept coming and coming until I thought it would never end. I didn't see his head, but I didn't have to; his body was enough to scare me bad.

Another person, Ernest Denks, named the monster "The Eater" when he first saw it because "it looked as if it could eat anything, anywhere, anytime." He described the beast: "a huge creature . . . that would probably weigh over a thousand pounds. This thing I saw looks like it had come from the ocean. It was gray, real long, and had a long pointed bone protruding from its forehead."

There was a rash of White River Monster sightings in 1971, and several citizens had presented a proposal to the board of directors of Newport. They wanted a stretch of the White River from Newport to Batesville declared as the "White River Monster Sanctuary and Refuge." A song had even been written about the creature—"The White River Monster Anthem."

In 1941, there appeared a new monster that became a competitor for space in the newspapers. This was Slimy Slim, a serpent in Lake Payette in Idaho. During July and August of that year, about thirty people saw the monster. Most of them were boating on the lake at the time; most of them did not believe their eyes. Finally, Thomas L. Rogers, the city attorney of Boise, told a reporter: "The serpent was about fifty feet long and going five miles an hour with a sort of undulating movement. . . . His head, which resembled that of a snub-nosed crocodile, was eight inches above the water. I'd say he was about thirty-five feet long, on consideration."

Almost immediately, hundreds of camera-carrying tourists descended on Lake Payette. Slim seemed to become shy after an article appeared about him in *Time* magazine. At any rate, little more was heard or seen of him.

South of Clifden in Connacht, Ireland, there is a bog-land in which a stream connects a chain of three small lakes, the largest one being Lough Fadda. In 1954, Mrs. Georgina Carberry was fishing with three friends on that lake. They saw "a black object which moved slowly, showing two humps. The head was about three feet out of water, in a long curve."

There were three other sightings of the Lough Fadda Monster. A man named Pat Walsh was in his boat when a head and neck emerged from the water. A family of seven watched "a black animal about twelve feet long," with a hump and neck. A local shepherd saw a monster on the land near the lake.

In the 1960s, Captain Lionel Leslie, an explorer, led an investigation of lake monsters in Ireland. In 1965, he went to Lough Fadda. There, hoping that a Peiste (a lake monster) would come to the surface to see what was going on, he exploded a small charge of gelignite against a rock. A few seconds later, a large black object came up about fifty yards from shore. The captain told a reporter from the *Irish Independent*: "I am satisfied beyond any doubt that there is a monster in Lough Fadda." He tried to net the creature, but with no success.

Ireland is also a hotbed of monsters—second only to Scotland. On May 18, 1960, three Roman Catholic priests, Daniel Murray, Matthew Burke, and Richard Quigly, were trout fishing on Lough Ree in the River Shannon. It was warm, the water was calm, and the fish were biting. Suddenly, they saw a large, flat-headed animal about one hundred yards away from where they were sitting.

One of them later said:

It went down under the water and came up again in the form of a loop. The length from the end of the coil to the head was six feet. There was about eighteen inches of head and neck over the water. The head and neck were narrow in comparison to the thickness of a good-sized salmon. It was getting its propulsion from underneath the water, and we did not see all of it.

Not to be outdone by the Scots and the Irish, the Russians said that a sea serpent was sighted in Siberia in 1965. Geologists that year reported seeing a huge animal twice at Lake Haiyr, near the Laptevykill Sea, in a region called Yakutia.

"The animal had a small head, a long, gleaming neck, jet-black skin, and a vertical fin on its back," said the report filed by these scientists. "That the lake is inhabited by a monster has long been known to the local population. Nobody would approach the lake because of it." The geologists who claimed to have seen the creature both on land and in the water brought back a sketch of the beast.

Finally, there may be a monster in the Washington, D. C. area. This one was seen by more than thirty people along the Chesapeake Bay in the summer of 1978. Nicknamed "Chessie," it seemed to have returned in 1980. But this time it was sighted in the Potomac River about sixty miles northeast of Richmond, Virginia.

Goodwin Muse, a farmer, and five friends were walking to the beach and saw a ten- to fourteen-foot-long monster in the water. Muse said: "I had spyglasses and was up on a bank eighteen feet high, and out thirty yards in the river you could see this long, dark streak in the water." The creature's body was "somewhat uniform in size, about as big around as a quart jar," and its head was "as large as my hand or more." He added: "Absolutely none of us drink."

The group watched the serpent for fifteen minutes and then it disappeared. John V. Merriner, a fishery scientist at the Virginia Institute of Marine Science was inclined to believe that it was a large, tropical snake. "I would lean toward an anaconda type," he said.

Monsters have been seen in lakes in France, Australia, Argentina, Ireland, Scotland, the Scandinavian countries, the United States, the Soviet Union, and many other countries. In the United States, there have been sightings in almost half of the states.

These creatures may be real animals that we have yet to classify. Too many sensible, seafaring people have seen them and too many scientists are looking for them for us to say for sure that they do not exist. If these stories and reports are just myths, why are scientists trying to unravel the mysteries surrounding them? It is too early to reject the possibility that monsters do—or even did—exist. In the meantime, why don't we keep our eyes and minds open?

Suggested Further READINGS

Aylesworth, Thomas G. *Werewolves and Other Monsters.* Reading, Massachusetts: Addison-Wesley Publishing Company, 1971.

Cohen, Daniel. *Monsters, Giants and Little Men from Mars.* Garden City, New York: Doubleday & Company, Incorporated, 1975.

Cooke, David C., and Cooke, Yvonne. *The Great Monster Hunt.* New York: W. W. Norton & Company, Incorporated, 1969.

Dinsdale, Tim. *Loch Ness Monster.* London: Routledge & Kegan Paul, 1961.

Gould, Rupert T. *The Loch Ness Monster.* New Hyde Park, New York: University Books, 1969.

Hall, Angus. *Monsters and Mythic Beasts.* Garden City, New York: Doubleday & Company, Incorporated, 1975.

121

Hill, Douglas, and Williams, Pat. *The Supernatural.* London: Aldus Books, 1965.

Landsburg, Alan. *In Search Of. . . .* Garden City, New York: Doubleday & Company, Incorporated, 1978.

Laycock, George. *Strange Monsters and Great Searches.* Garden City, New York: Doubleday & Company, Incorporated, 1973.

Spence, Lewis. *An Encyclopaedia of Occultism.* New Hyde Park, New York: University Books, 1960.

Thompson, C. J. S. *The Mystery and Lore of Monsters.* New Hyde Park, New York: University Books, 1968.

World Almanac Book of the Strange, The. New York: New American Library, 1977.

ABOUT THE AUTHOR

THOMAS G. AYLESWORTH, who has a Ph.D., taught at Michigan State University and in the public schools in Michigan, Illinois, and Indiana. He is the author of more than thirty books, including *Understanding Body Talk, The World of Microbes,* and *Storm Alert.* Mr. Aylesworth is presently an editor with a publishing house.